This book must be returned by the date specified at the time of issue as the DATE DUE FOR RETURN.

The loan may be extended (personally, by post, telephone or online) for a further period if the book is not required by another reader, by quoting the above number / author / title.

Enquiries: 01709 336774

www.rotherham.gov.uk/libraries

MAKE YOUR OWN

Jams, Chutneys and Pickles

OVER 80 EASY-TO-FOLLOW RECIPES

*** Mary Ford ***

Michael O'Mara Books Limited

First published in Great Britain in 2013 by
Michael O'Mara Books Limited
9 Lion Yard
Tremadoc Road
London SW4 7NQ

A CIP catalogue record for this book is available from the British Library.

Papers used by Michael O'Mara Books Limited are natural, recyclable products made from wood grown in sustainable forests. The manufacturing processes conform to the environmental regulations of the country of origin.

ISBN: 978-1-78243-108-4 in hardback print format
ISBN: 978-1-78243-169-5 in ebook format

1 2 3 4 5 6 7 8 9 10

Illustrations by Aubrey Smith
Cover design by Ana Bjezancevic
Typeset by K.DESIGN, Winscombe, Somerset
Printed and bound by CPI Group (UK) Ltd, Croydon, CR0 4YY

www.mombooks.com

CONTENTS

CONVERSION TABLES

~ↄ˄ᴑ~

onversions are approximate. Ensure you follow only one set of measurements, either metric or imperial, per recipe.

~ↄᴑ~ Weight ~ↄᴑ~

Metric	Imperial
15 g	½ oz
25 g	1 oz
40 g	1½ oz
50 g	2 oz
85 g	3 oz
115 g	4 oz
145 g	5 oz
175 g	6 oz
200 g	7 oz
225 g	8 oz
250 g	9 oz
285 g	10 oz

Metric	Imperial
350 g	12 oz
375 g	13 oz
400 g	14 oz
425 g	15 oz
450 g	1 lb
550 g	1¼ lb
675 g	1½ lb
750 g	1¾ lb
900 g	2 lb
1.3 kg	3 lb
1.8 kg	4 lb
2.25 kg	5 lb

～⚭～ **Measurements** ～⚭～

Metric	Imperial
5 mm	¼ inch
1 cm	½ inch
2.5 cm	1 inch
5 cm	2 inch
7.5 cm	3 inch
10 cm	4 inch
12.5 cm	5 inch
15 cm	6 inch
18 cm	7 inch
20 cm	8 inch
23 cm	9 inch
25 cm	10 inch
30 cm	12 inch

~o⌐ Liquids ~o⌐

Metric	Imperial
15 ml	½ fl oz
25 ml	1 fl oz
50 ml	2 fl oz
75 ml	3 fl oz
100 ml	3½ fl oz
125 ml	4 fl oz
150 ml	5 fl oz/¼ pint
175 ml	6 fl oz
200 ml	7 fl oz
225 ml	8 fl oz
250 ml	9 fl oz
300 ml	10 fl oz/½ pint
350 ml	12 fl oz
400 ml	14 fl oz
450 ml	16 fl oz/¾ pint
500 ml	18 fl oz

Metric	Imperial
568 ml	20 fl oz/1 pint
600 ml	1 pint milk
700 ml	1¼ pints
850 ml	1½ pints
1 litre	1¾ pints
1.2 litres	2 pints
1.3 litres	2¼ pints
1.4 litres	2½ pints
1.5 litres	2¾ pints
1.7 litres	3 pints
1.8 litres	3¼ pints
2 litres	3½ pints
2.5 litres	4½ pints
2.8 litres	5 pints
3 litres	5¼ pints

ᴓᴓ US Cups ᴓᴓ

¼ cup	60 ml
⅓ cup	70 ml
½ cup	125 ml
⅔ cup	150 ml
¾ cup	175 ml
1 cup	250 ml
1½ cups	375 ml
2 cups	500 ml
3 cups	750 ml
4 cups	1 litre
6 cups	1.5 litres

ᴓᴓ Spoons ᴓᴓ

Metric	Imperial
1.25 ml	¼ teaspoon
2.5 ml	½ teaspoon
5 ml	1 teaspoon
10 ml	2 teaspoons
15 ml	3 teaspoons/1 tablespoon
30 ml	2 tablespoons
45 ml	3 tablespoons
60 ml	4 tablespoons
75 ml	5 tablespoons
90 ml	6 tablespoons

INTRODUCTION

ᴡelcome to the wonderful world of preserves. There is nothing quite like slathering a dollop of beautiful homemade jam on a slice of toast, or eating a chunk of cheese with a generous helping of pickle made by your own fair hands. The supermarkets are of course teeming with cheap and tasty commercial preserves, but none of these compare to the beauty and exquisite taste of the homemade varieties. In this selection of recipes for delectable jams, jellies, pickles and chutneys you'll be spoilt for choice.

As people have turned their backs on convenience food and looked towards more healthy and economical ways of eating, home cooking has never been more popular. And what better place to start than with your store cupboard? A well-stocked larder is essential for any lover of food, and the recipes contained in this book will allow you to arm yourself with the basics and beyond. Don't forget that any leftover jars can be given as beautiful gifts.

The art of preserving necessitates using fruits and vegetables in season and at their most ripe. This offers you the chance to save money and get yourself a refreshing breath of air by going blackberry picking or foraging for berries. Otherwise you can raid your greengrocers for supplies of seasonal and, if you can, local produce. If you find you don't have enough time to use fruits and vegetables when they are in season, turn to page 29 for handy hints on freezing.

Make Your Own Jams, Chutneys and Pickles has been designed to appeal to both the experienced and novice cook. Whether you are in the market for a traditional Seville orange marmalade, or if you fancy trying something completely different, such as a gooseberry relish, this book offers a range of tasty treats.

Regardless of any previous experience you might have had of cooking preserves, always be mindful of your health and safety as the ingredients reach very high temperatures. The sugars in jam can get especially hot, so make sure you use a large enough pan and keep an eye out for any mixture spitting. Be especially careful when transferring the preserves from the pan into a measuring jug – make sure you wear oven gloves. Line up your jars ahead of transferring the liquid, and move any small children and animals out of harm's way.

With something to suit every palate, this collection of delicious jams, chutneys and pickles guarantees a failsafe and thoroughly enjoyable sojourn into the world of preserves. Now it's time to get cracking!

TIPS AND TOOLS

When preserving, preparation is essential. Whether it's stockpiling jam jars or making sure you leave your chutney long enough before you can eat it, planning ahead is key. This chapter gathers together all of the essential information you will need before commencing.

Essential Equipment

All of the recipes in this book can be made using everyday kitchen equipment, although experienced jam-makers who make large quantities of preserves may want to invest in a large, stainless steel preserving pan and a jam thermometer. Many preserve-making items, such as jelly bags, can be quickly improvised from equipment already in the kitchen. For instance, a sieve could form the basis of a jelly bag, or you could use a cheese grater to remove lemon peel. As ever, it pays to be prepared, so make sure your equipment is clean and to hand when you need it.

Saucepans

It is essential that the saucepan is large enough to allow the contents to boil and rise up in the pan. A heavy base is required to prevent burning so stainless steel pans are ideal. Brass, copper, iron and chipped enamel saucepans should be avoided as they may burn or taint the finished product and they should never be used with vinegar – the vinegar reacts with the metal, which gives a strange flavour to the finished preserve. You can use brass or copper pans for making jams, but be warned the finished product will contain less vitamin C than those made in a stainless steel pan. Brass or copper also imparts a green colour to gooseberry jam, which otherwise goes brownish-yellow, but a few drops of commercial food colouring will rectify this.

Food Processor (or Mincer)

Very useful for breaking up hard-skinned fruits, which results in a shorter boiling time required to soften the skins. Less water is then needed, cutting the cooking time and resulting in a better flavour. A processor can also be used for preparing fruit and vegetables for chutneys. If the recipe calls for it, roughly chopped fruit or vegetables could be cooked and then processed until smooth.

Measuring Jug

Plastic, glass, earthenware or stainless steel measuring jugs are equally suitable. Other metals should be avoided, particularly if vinegar is being used. Also essential for transferring your preserve into jars.

Spoons

Use a wooden spoon for stirring, particularly where acids are involved. A stainless steel slotted spoon is good for skimming and removing stones and pips.

Thermometer

A good quality sugar thermometer which goes above 105°C (220°F) is useful in jam making. They are widely available so it should be very easy to get hold of one. Always store thermometers in an upright position, and never lay a hot thermometer down as it can cause the mercury to split. Keep the thermometer in a jug of warm water next to the cooker and replace after use.

Sieves

Plastic or stainless steel sieves should be used to avoid tainting.

Jelly Bag

The fine cloth of these helps to strain juices from cooked fruit pulp – perfect for making jelly. Purpose-made jelly bags (not wine straining bags) may be purchased but a jelly bag could be improvised from a suitable close woven (but not muslin) cloth. A jelly bag for small quantities can be improvised by placing a suitable cloth in a large sieve.

Splash Guard

Some chutneys can spit and a splash guard may prove useful.

Jars and Lids

Clean, dry glass jars should be used. Commercial jars can be reused but must always be thoroughly cleaned first. Lids must be airtight and screw-top jars, such as honey or coffee jars, are unsuitable as they are not airtight. Ask friends and family to save old jars for you so you'll never be short when the time comes to make your preserves.

Lids used for pickles or chutneys must be vinegar protected either with fully lacquered insides, or be manufactured from plastic material. If in doubt, do not reuse lids.

Waxed Discs

Place wax-side down on top of the jam before putting the lid on and they help to preserve your produce by keeping out air and moisture. They are widely available online or in kitchen shops.

Mary's Tip

Waxed discs are not vinegar proof so are not, therefore, suitable for chutneys and pickles, and anything else that contains vinegar.

Labels

Home-made jams, chutneys and pickles make lovely presents, particularly when decorated with an illustrated label and jar cover. You can create your own labels using good, old-fashioned paper and sellotape or you can buy self-adhesive labels – some of which are very pretty – both online and on the high street. Remember to always date and label jars when the filling is cold.

Knives

It is always good to have a range of different knives on hand. Sharp stainless steel kitchen knives are required for peeling and chopping ingredients, and small, serrated knives are often good for slicing.

Methylated Spirit

This is used for the pectin test and for polishing jars for shows. It should be stored in a tightly fitting screw-top jar or bottle, away from heat sources and out of reach of children.

Muslin

Used to make spice or herb bags, and particularly useful for wrapping around pith and pips when making marmalade. Muslin should not be used as a substitute for a jelly bag.

Grater

A very useful tool when making preserves; even better if it has three grades of grating.

~ Ingredients ~

The general rule is to pick top-quality fruits and vegetables for making your preserves. They should be ripe and at the peak of their flavour.

Sugar

Granulated sugar is perfectly adequate for all of the recipes in this book but more expensive, specialized preserving sugars can be used without the need to adjust recipes. Pectin sugars, however, should be used according to the manufacturer's recipes and should not be substituted for granulated sugar for these recipes.

Soft, dark sugar makes a rich chutney, while granulated sugar is preferable for light-coloured chutney. Demerara sugar gives a crunchy texture.

Vinegar

Only the best quality white or brown malt vinegar with an acetic acid content of 5 per cent should be used. Some draught vinegars may have a lower acetic acid content and are best avoided.

Wine or herb vinegars can be used to add a delicacy of flavour. Chopped garlic or sprigs of fresh herbs are added to the basic vinegar and left to steep. Herbs picked just before flowering give maximum flavour.

Spiced vinegars can be purchased or prepared at home. Suitable spices for vinegar include cinnamon bark, cloves, peppercorns, cayenne pepper, mace and whole allspice. All you need to do is place the pickling spices in the vinegar, stir, leave for 1–2 months, strain and then bottle.

Fruit-flavoured vinegars can be made from soft fruits such as blackcurrants and raspberries. To each 450 g (1 lb) of ripe fruit add 600 ml (1 pint) of best malt vinegar, place in a glass or china bowl and cover with a cloth and allow to stand for 3–5 days, stirring occasionally. Drain off the liquid 10 minutes before bottling. Sugar may be omitted and the vinegar sweetened prior to use if preferred.

Salt

Essential for making pickles as it dehydrates the vegetables, leaving them crisp and crunchy.

Fruit and Vegetables

The finest quality, freshly picked fruit and vegetables should always be used for jams and jellies. Look out for unwaxed citrus fruit if you need to use the peel and always give citrus fruit a good wash before using to remove any residual spray. A dash of washing-up liquid followed by a very good rinse should suffice.

Choose fresh vegetables for pickling, although lower grade, but not mouldy, fruit and vegetables can be used for chutneys.

Mary's Tip

Always keep aside the peel from citrus fruits as it makes great marmalade. Make sure you scrub the fruit well beforehand, peel it and then bag it up and store it in the freezer for use at a later date. Remember to use extra fruit when you come to make your marmalade as frozen fruit contains less pectin (see page 26).

Spices

Ground spices can be used for chutneys but whole spices must be used for spicing vinegar as this avoids cloudiness. If whole spices are to be included in chutney, they should be crushed and tied in muslin before use.

❧ How to Reach a Good Set ❧

The right combination of sugar, pectin and acids is essential for making sure your jams, jellies and marmalades reach a good set. Although certain fruits are known to contain more pectin or acid than others, different factors – such as the season, variety, freshness, ripeness of the fruit – mean these levels can fluctuate at any one time. This explains why a preserve might react slightly differently each time you make it, even though you have used the same recipe.

Pectin

Pectin is generally found in the walls of fruit and it is the essential component of jam making as it is the substance that makes the jam set. The more pectin a fruit contains, the more sugar it will set. Under-ripe fruits tend to contain the most pectin, while over-ripe fruits and fruit picked after a bout of wet weather are generally lower in pectin.

'Good' pectin content will set 340 g (12 oz) fruit to 450 g (1 lb) sugar. 'Medium' pectin will set 450 g (1 lb) fruit to 450 g (1 lb) sugar. If medium pectin is present, the fruit should be simmered for a little longer to evaporate off more water, and a further test carried out (see below). If pectin is still on the low side, it signifies the fruit is deficient and the sugar should be reduced by 115 g (4 oz) to 450 g (1 lb) of fruit. 'Low' pectin is unlikely to set and extra pectin should be added.

A pectin test must always be carried out when specified in a recipe. Low and high pectin fruits, blended together, improve the setting qualities of jam.

Pectin Test

This test shows the quantity of pectin present in fruit. The more pectin there is in fruit, the more sugar it will set.

Use one teaspoon of the juice formed after simmering the jam or marmalade, pour into a glass and leave to cool. Add 3 teaspoons of methylated spirit.

26

Pectin Content

This list shows you what's what in terms of pectin content.

Good:	Medium:	Poor:
Blackcurrants	Fresh apricots	Late
Redcurrants	Early	blackberries
Cooking apples	blackberries	Cherries
Crab apples	Greengages	Elderberries
Damsons	Loganberries	Marrow
Gooseberries	Raspberries	Pears
Some plums		Rhubarb
Quince		Strawberries
		Vegetables

Shake the glass gently and leave to stand for 1 minute. If plenty of pectin is present, a transparent jelly-like lump will be formed.

If the pectin is poor, the jam will not set without extra pectin; for medium pectin, boil a little longer; if your pectin is good then your jam will set well.

Mary's Tip

Although commercial pectin is available, you can make your own by placing windfall apples or redcurrants in a saucepan with enough water to cover. Bring to the boil and then simmer for approximately 20 or 30 minutes, or until the fruit is soft. Strain off the juice and freeze until required.

Acid

This is an essential ingredient of jam making. Low acid fruits require extra acid, in the form of lemon juice, citric or tartaric acid. This is added as the fruit is cooked in order to extract the pectin. Each 1.75 kg (4 lb) of fruit requires an average of 2 tablespoons of lemon juice, or ¼ teaspoon of citric or tartaric acid. Alternatively, 150 ml (¼ pint) of redcurrant or gooseberry juice may be used. Vegetables contain practically no acid and if vegetables such as marrows are used for jams, then extra acid should always be added.

Acid Content

This list shows you what's what in terms of acid content.

Low:	High:
Sweet apples	Cooking apples
Late blackberries	Crab apples
Cherries	Blackcurrants
Pears	Redcurrants
Strawberries	Damsons
Vegetables	Dessert gooseberries
	Lemons
	Seville oranges
	Grapefruit

The extra acid should be added at the commencement of the cooking process to fully extract the pectin and recipes should always be followed exactly in order to achieve the correct proportions of fruit, sugar and pectin for perfect results.

～ Freezing Fruits and ～ Vegetables

The judicious use of the freezer can prolong the jam- and chutney-making season without impairing the flavour or quality of the finished product. It's especially useful when there is a glut of fruit or vegetables in the garden, or in order to take advantage of special offers at the supermarket.

The produce chosen for freezing must be in peak condition and frozen as soon as possible. Vegetables and some fruits need carefully timed blanching and cooling prior to freezing (see pages 30–35).

Most fruit and vegetables are frozen in heavy duty polythene bags from which the air is extracted. The bag, which should be appropriately labelled, should then be placed in an empty, clean Tupperware tub. Metal or foil containers should not be used for freezing fruit or vegetables.

When you come to use the frozen produce, most fruits and vegetables can be cooked from frozen, although citrus fruits should be covered with boiling water while still frozen, and then sliced and cooked immediately to minimize discolouration.

It is important to remember that freezing lowers the pectin content of fruit slightly, particularly strawberries, and an extra one-eighth weight of fruit may be added to the recipe. A pectin test should always be carried out on jam made from frozen fruit and additional pectin stock (see page 27) added if necessary.

Mary's Tip
Freezing is not suitable for vegetables or fruits for pickling as these will quickly lose their crispness.

Step-by-Step Instructions for Freezing Vegetables

Equipment
saucepan with lid
blanching basket or wire sieve
150 gauge polythene bags with labels
and sealing strips

1. Put a large saucepan of water on to boil.

2. Wash the vegetables and peel and de-seed if necessary. Cut into even-sized chunks.

3. Place the vegetables in a sieve or blanching basket and immerse in boiling water.

4. Bring the water back to the boil within 1 minute. Hard boil for 1 minute, or as directed in the table below, with the lid on.

5. Place a big handful of ice cubes in a large bowl and fill with cold water.

6. Immediately remove the sieve and plunge into the iced water until cool.

7. Drain and place on a clean tea cloth to dry.

8. Pack loosely into polythene bags and seal with a freezer tie.

9. Label, spread bag out flat and freeze immediately. Shake occasionally for the first hour of freezing to keep the vegetables free flowing.

How to Freeze Fruits and Vegetables

FRUIT/VEG	PREPARATION	BLANCHING	CONTAINER
Apples	Peel, core and slice (keep in water with lemon juice added until ready to freeze)	1–2 minutes and cool in chilled water	Freeze in polythene bags or rigid container
Apricots	Wash and stone	Scald in boiling water for 1–2 minutes	Freeze in polythene bags

FRUIT/VEG	PREPARATION	BLANCHING	CONTAINER
Aubergines	Peel and slice thickly	4 minutes	Freeze in polythene bags
Bananas	Unsuitable for freezing		
Beetroot	Wash carefully and boil until tender. Rub off skins. Slice or dice	None	Freeze in container
Blackberries	Wash, if necessary, and dry	None	Freeze in polythene trays or bags
Blueberries	As for blackberries		
Cabbage	Unsuitable for freezing if used for pickles		
Carrots	Peel, wash and dry. Large carrots can be sliced	4 minutes	Freeze in polythene bags
Cauliflower	Break into small florets and wash	3 minutes	Freeze in polythene bags
Cherries	Drain and stone. Stand in chilled water for 1 hour	None	Freeze in polythene trays or bags
Courgettes	Trim and slice	1 minute	Freeze in polythene bags

FRUIT/VEG	PREPARATION	BLANCHING	CONTAINER
Damsons	Wash in chilled water with lemon juice added. Stone if required and dry	None	Freeze in polythene bags or rigid containers
French beans	Top and tail. Cut large beans in half	2–3 minutes	Freeze in polythene bags
Gooseberries	Top and tail, wash in chilled water and dry thoroughly	None	Freeze in polythene trays or bags
Herbs	Wash and dry	None	Freeze in polythene bags
Logan-berries	Rinse in chilled water. Drain and dry	None	Freeze in polythene trays or bags
Marrow	Unsuitable for freezing		
Melon	Peel, remove seeds and cube	None	Freeze in polythene bags or rigid containers
Mulberries	Rinse in chilled water, drain and dry	None	Freeze in polythene bags or rigid containers
Nectarines	Unsuitable for freezing for jams		
Onions	Unsuitable for freezing if used for pickles		

FRUIT/VEG	PREPARATION	BLANCHING	CONTAINER
Peaches	Unsuitable for freezing for jams		
Pears	Unsuitable for freezing		
Peppers	Wash, de-seed and slice	2 minutes	Freeze in polythene bags
Plums and gages	Wash and stone if required	Scald for 1–2 minutes	Freeze in polythene bags
Pumpkin	Not recommended for freezing		
Quince	Peel, core and slice. Simmer until tender and drain	None	Freeze in polythene bags
Raspberries	Hull, if necessary, wash and dry	None	Freeze in polythene bags or rigid containers
Red and black-currants	Strip from stalks, wash and drain (jelly-making does not require stalks to be removed)	None	Freeze in polythene trays or bags
Rhubarb	Wash and trim the stalks into 2.5 cm (1 in) chunks	1–2 minutes	Freeze in polythene trays or bags
Runner beans	String and slice	1 minute	Freeze in polythene bags

FRUIT/VEG	PREPARATION	BLANCHING	CONTAINER
Seville oranges	Scrub thoroughly to remove impurities	None. Use as soon as possible	Freeze whole in polythene bags
Strawberries	Hull, wash and dry fruit	None	Freeze in trays or bags
Sweetcorn	Remove outer husks	4–6 minutes	Freeze individually in polythene bags
Tomatoes	Wipe	None	Pack whole into polythene bags
Zucchini	See courgette		

⤜ Techniques ⤛

Making preserves is, generally speaking, a straight-forward process. Don't feel daunted by this list of techniques – there are few involved, and they are easy to master.

Preparing Fruit

Look out for unwaxed citrus fruit if you need to use the peel and always give citrus fruit a good wash before using to remove any residual spray. Warm citrus fruit in the microwave for 30 seconds, or cover with boiling water for a few minutes, before juicing it as this helps to extract the maximum amount of juice. Peel can be removed in one of three ways, depending on what the recipe calls for. You can use a zester if you only need a small amount; if the recipe calls for lots of peel, use a grater; if you need to remove it in big strips then use a vegetable peeler.

Brushing Down

To avoid crystallization, brush any sugar crystals from the side of the pan and the spoon with a wet pastry brush.

Rolling Boil

Jam should be kept at a hard, rolling boil after the sugar has dissolved, causing the mixture to rise in the pan.

Skimming

Draw the 'scum' to one side with a spoon and remove. This will improve the finished appearance of the jam.

Testing if Chutney is Ready

Draw a spoon across the top of the mixture. The track should be clear of free-running vinegar. If liquid is present, boil for a little longer.

Jam: Testing for Set

There are three ways you can test your jam for set:

1. A thermometer: dip a thermometer into
hot water and then place it in the jam. If the
temperature reaches 105°C/220°F the jam
is set. Make sure you stir the jam thoroughly
before taking the temperature.

2. The cold saucer test: remove the pan from
the heat. Cool a scant teaspoon of jam on a
cold plate. The jam should set and form a
skin, which will wrinkle when pushed.

3. The flake test: remove the pan from the heat.
Dip in a wooden spoon, remove it and allow
to cool slightly. If the jam is ready, it will form
a 'skirt', or flakes, on the spoon as it drops. If
the jam is not ready, it will run off the spoon.
If this happens, the jam should be boiled for a
few minutes more and tested again.

Preparing Jars

It is essential you prepare the jars before filling them
to ensure you have eliminated any contamination. If
you are reusing old jars, check for cracks and wash off
old labels in a bowl of soapy water.

Thoroughly wash and rinse the jars, drain and place
in a cold oven. Heat the oven to 160°C/325°F/gas 3
for 10 minutes or until the jars are dry. Jars should be

warm when you fill them, but make sure they are not hot as the heat can cause peel to rise.

Mary's Tip
A dishwasher is ideal for cleaning and sterilizing jars and bottles.

Filling Jars

Once your preserve is ready, transfer it carefully into a measuring jug, making sure you wear oven gloves for protection. Line up your warm jars and pour in the preserve. Fill to within 3 mm (⅛ in) of the jar's rim – too much air at the top encourages the growth of mould. Cover and wipe immediately. Leave the jars to stand until cold. Once cool, label them clearly (see page 40) and store in a cool, dark, well-ventilated place.

Pickles should be packed loosely to allow the vinegar to penetrate. Always ensure that all vegetables are submerged.

Waxed discs should be placed immediately onto hot jam (they are not suitable for chutneys and pickles). Cellophane covers, moistened on the upper side, should be placed on jars immediately.

Removing Bubbles

Once potted, use a knife or a small, long-handled wooden spoon to remove air bubbles from the chutney or pickles.

Labelling

Always date and label jars when the filling is cold. When labelling jams, chutney or pickles it is always helpful to indicate their 'ready by' or 'use by' dates.

⋙ Preserving SOS ⋘

Even the most experienced maker of preserves faces difficulties. Problems usually occur when the recipe is not followed exactly, or when over-ripe fruit is used.

Why is there mould on my jam?

You might have followed an incorrect procedure for covering, or it could be due to a lack of hygiene during the preparation of the fruit and containers. Poor storage conditions or too much air space at the top of the jar can also account for mould. When storing any preserve, do not keep in a cupboard over a microwave, refrigerator, washing machine or other source of heat.

Why does jam crystallize?

Make sure you don't under or over boil the ingredients and ensure the pan is brushed down (see page 36). Check you've used the right amount of ingredients – crystallization can be caused by an imbalance in the recipe. Weak or over-acid content can also be to blame.

Why hasn't the jam set?

This could be for several reasons:

- A lack of pectin. See page 26 for more on pectin.

- You might not have boiled off enough water before the sugar was added. Or, alternatively, you might not have boiled the ingredients for long enough after the sugar was added.

- The quantities of ingredients might be unbalanced.

Always remember that if the setting point has not been reached 20 minutes after the sugar has been added, then further boiling will not improve the set.

Why have the contents shrunk?

This could be down to one of three reasons: you might have over boiled the liquid, the pan lid might not have provided adequate covering (vinegar can evaporate if the lid is not airtight), or your storage was a little on the warm side.

Why is my jelly cloudy?

It's important to wash fruit thoroughly before commencing with your preserves as using dirty fruit will lead to a cloudy finish when making jelly. You should also ensure the mesh of your jelly bag is sufficiently close knit, and should always avoid squeezing the bag to hasten drainage.

Why is the jam 'weeping'?

This is normally down to too much acid.

Why are the fruit or vegetable skins and peel too tough?

This could either be the result of insufficient simmering in enough water to soften the skins before addition of the sugar, or over-boiling once the sugar has been added.

Why does my pickle lack 'bite'?

You might not have allowed your pickle sufficient time to mature, or this might be down to the use of poor quality vinegar.

Why is my preserve discoloured?

Always remember to wash fruit and vegetables thoroughly before you begin cooking. Discolouration might be down to insufficient brining to reduce moisture in produce, or the use of ground spices instead of whole.

Mary's Tip

Local produce shows remain very popular and provide an opportunity for recognition of expertise and for constructive criticism of jam or pickles.
Remember to read schedules carefully and always take notice of size of jars, types of jam etc. if you intend to enter your produce.
Presentation is very important – jars should be absolutely clean and free from fingerprints and lids must be appropriate to the contents, i.e. pickles must have an airtight, vinegar-proof lid.

What the judges look for:

Jams, jellies, marmalades: bright, sparkling preserve and a well-filled jar. If a waxed disc is used, this must fit completely over the surface with no trapped air bubbles. No mould or crystallizing round the edges; adequate set and good, appropriate texture; tender, not hard, fruit or peel; good, clean, distinctive fruit flavour and aroma. Jellies should be clear when the pot is held up to the light, with no cloudiness; marmalades should display a skilful, traditional hand cutting of the peel.

Chutneys: a mature, mellow flavour and a smooth but interesting texture (not just a pulp), with no loose vinegar.

Pickles: mature but with a bite and crispness. The contents should be nicely packed and well submerged in vinegar. Onions should be evenly matched in size and neatly trimmed. They should be crisp but with the vinegar penetrating to the middle.

MARMALADES

ᴕᴑᴖ

With a distinctive, bitter flavour and, traditionally, a short window in which to make it, marmalade is revered among preserve connoisseurs. Traditionally, marmalade is made from Seville oranges, although modern variations can contain all of the citrus fruits alongside more unusual ingredients. If using citrus fruits, remove their wax coating prior to use by pouring boiling water over the fruit and scrubbing. Look out for unwaxed fruits, but remember to carefully wash and dry all fruit prior to use.

Traditional marmalade can range in colour from thick and dark to a light, translucent appearance. The texture of marmalade is a matter of individual taste. The peel may be grated, minced, chopped or processed in a food processer, or it can also be cooked, with roughly one third sliced and the remainder liquidized in a little of the juice. Whatever your preference, remember to keep notes on the way the peel has been processed.

Fresh, whole frozen, or ready-pulped fruit can be used for marmalade. If using whole frozen citrus fruit an extra one-eighth weight fruit should be added to the recipe to compensate for any loss of pectin. The fruit should be cooked gently from frozen with the amount of water specified in the recipe in a tightly-lidded saucepan as thawing can discolour the fruit.

Alternatively, the frozen oranges can be left to stand in a bowl of boiling water for 10 minutes. The oranges should then be cut into halves and the flesh scooped out. It's possible to remove the pips very easily by gently squeezing the frozen flesh. The skin can be chopped, using a sharp knife, and the orange should be cooked immediately in boiling water to prevent discolouration.

The saucepan used for marmalade making should ideally have a heavy base and really thick sides. The pan should be made from or coated with an acid-resistant material such as stainless steel, aluminium or enamel because acid will react with copper, iron or brass to impair the flavour of the finished product.

Just as with jam making, the pectin and acid content of fruits used for marmalade is important in order to obtain a good set. Most of the pectin in citrus fruit is in the pips and pith so these should always be used. Extra acid in the form of lemon juice is added to Seville orange marmalade to balance the high pectin content. As ever, recipes should be followed carefully, with a pectin test carried out where necessary. When potting marmalade, it's important to remember that over-hot jars may cause the peel to rise.

46

⦿ Three-Seasons Marmalade ⦿

A bittersweet combination of grapefruit, lemon and orange that can be made any time of the year.

juice, peel and pith of 2 lemons
juice, peel and pith of 1 sweet orange
juice, peel and pith (if thick enough) of
1 medium-sized grapefruit

(total weight of all three fruits =
approximately 450 g (1 lb))

1.5–2 litres (2½–3½ pints) water
1.5 kg (3 lb) granulated sugar

1. Prepare the jars (see page 38).

2. Place the pith, pips and any blemished pieces of peel into a muslin cloth and secure with a piece of string.

3. Chop the peel into strips of the required size and place in the preserving pan, together with the muslin bag. Pour in the water and the fruit juice.

4. Simmer the contents of the pan without a lid for approximately 2 hours, or until the peel is tender and the liquid has reduced. Once the peel is tender, test a little of the liquid for pectin (see page 26). Remove the bag and squeeze it well into the pan. Discard the bag and contents.

5. Pour the granulated sugar into the pan and stir well using a wooden spoon. Continue stirring over a low heat until the sugar is dissolved, remembering to brush down the sides of the pan (see page 36). Rapidly boil the contents of the pan until setting point is reached.

6. To test if the marmalade has set, spoon a small amount onto a chilled saucer or conduct a flake test (see page 38). Skim the top (see page 37) and then pour the boiling marmalade into jars and fill to 3 mm (⅛ in) below the brim. Wipe the outside and leave to cool, then label, date and store (see page 40).

Mary's Tip
This tasty marmalade will be ready to eat after 24 hours.

✎ Seville Orange Marmalade ✎

This is a classic marmalade, and you can always freeze the fruits to give you the option of making it any time of the year (see page 29).

juice, peel and pith of 450 g (1 lb) Seville oranges
juice of 1 small lemon
1.5–2 litres (2½–3½ pints) water
900 g (2 lb) granulated sugar

1. Prepare the jars.

2. Place a large strainer over a bowl and line it with muslin. Pour the juice from the orange and lemon, together with the pips into the muslin. Add the pith and any blemished peel from the orange. Secure the muslin cloth with a piece of string.

3. Chop the orange peel into strips of the required size.

4. Place the peel and the muslin bag into an open pan. Pour in the water and the fruit juice and boil for approximately 2 hours, or until the peel is tender. Once the peel is tender, test a little of the liquid for pectin. Remove the bag and squeeze it well into the pan. Discard the bag and its contents.

5. Pour the sugar into the pan and stir well using a wooden spoon. Continue stirring over a low heat until the sugar is dissolved, remembering to brush down the sides of the pan.

6. Rapidly boil the contents of the pan until setting point is reached.

7. To test if the marmalade has set, spoon a small amount onto a chilled saucer or conduct a flake test. Skim the top and then pour the boiling marmalade into jars and fill to 3 mm (⅛ in) below the brim. Wipe the outside and leave to cool, then label, date and store.

Mary's Tip
Orange pith contains lots of pectin, so make sure not to discard any.

ᴐᴑ *Quince Marmalade* ᴐᴑ

Marmalade was traditionally made with quinces, a fragrant pear-like fruit that is best eaten cooked.

450 g (1 lb) quinces, roughly chopped
approximately 600 ml (1 pint) water
900 g (2 lb) quinces, peeled, cored and sliced
680 g (1½ lb) granulated sugar

1. Prepare the jars (see page 38).

2. Cover the roughly chopped quinces with the water and boil until soft. Strain and reserve 600 ml (1 pint) juice.

3. Place the juice in a heavy saucepan with the peeled, cored and sliced quinces. Cover with a tightly fitting lid and simmer until the fruit is tender.

4. Pass through a coarse sieve or food processor, and then boil until an almost dry paste is formed. Add the sugar and, stirring continuously, boil for 30 minutes. The marmalade will be very firm and bright in colour. Pot and seal immediately.

Mary's Tip
The roughly chopped quinces can be of an inferior quality to the peeled, cored and sliced quinces.

～ Redcurrant Marmalade ～

This tart berry makes an excellent marmalade.

2 sweet oranges, thinly sliced
water, as required
680 g (1½ lb) redcurrants
680 g (1½ lb) raisins
680 g (1½ lb) granulated sugar

1. Prepare the jars (see page 38).

2. Place the oranges in a pan with sufficient water to barely cover. Simmer until peel is tender.

3. Add the fruit and simmer until tender. Add the sugar and bring gently to the boil, stirring until the sugar is dissolved. Boil until setting point is reached (see page 38). Pot and seal immediately.

༻ Rhubarb Marmalade ༺

Tasty and tangy, rhubarb grows best in warm temperatures, so tends to thrive during the summer; a forcer can be used to help the plant along during the winter months.

peel of 1 lemon
peel of 1 Seville orange
450 ml (¾ pint) water
680 g (1½ lb) rhubarb, chopped
½ teaspoon tartaric acid
680 g (1½ lb) granulated sugar

1. Prepare the jars (see page 38).

2. Cut the peel of the lemon and orange into strips and squeeze and strain the juice.

3. Remove pith from fruit, cut into strips and tie it up into a muslin bag, along with the pips. Soak the bag, peel and juice for 12 hours in 300 ml (½ pint) water.

4. Place the bag, peel and water in a saucepan and simmer with the lid on until the peel is tender, pressing the bag from time to time.

5. When the peel is tender, add the rhubarb, remaining water and tartaric acid. Cook gently, stirring occasionally until the fruit becomes a thick pulp.

6. Remove the bag, squeezing well. Add the sugar, stir until dissolved, then boil for 10 minutes or until setting point is reached (see page 38). Pot and seal immediately.

∽ Pumpkin Marmalade ∽

This is a thick and tasty alternative to traditional marmalade.

2 Seville oranges, thinly sliced
450 ml (¾ pint) water
900 g (2 lb) ripe pumpkin, chopped into small cubes
900 g (2 lb) granulated sugar

1. Prepare the jars (see page 38).

2. Cover the oranges with the water and cover the pumpkin with the sugar and leave both to stand for 24 hours.

3. Place the oranges and the water they have been soaking in in a large pan. Bring to the boil and simmer until tender. Add the pumpkin and the sugar and simmer until the sugar has dissolved and the pumpkin is tender, then boil until setting point is reached (see page 38). Pot and seal immediately.

Mary's Tip
Ensure you wash and dry hard fruit and vegetables thoroughly immediately before use as this will result in a cleaner and brighter product.

∙⊙∙ Seville Orange and ∙⊙∙ Whisky Marmalade

A grown-up version of the traditional Seville orange marmalade. You won't be able to resist its kick.

450 g (1 lb) Seville oranges, scrubbed and juiced
1 small lemon, scrubbed and juiced
1.5–2 litres (2½–3½ pints) water
900 g (2 lb) granulated sugar
3 tablespoons whisky

1. Prepare the jars (see page 38).

2. Place a large strainer over a bowl and line it with muslin. Pour the juice, together with the pips, into the muslin. Remove the pith and place it in the muslin, together with any blemished peel. Secure the muslin cloth with a piece of string.

3. Chop the peel into strips of the required size.

4. Place the peel and the muslin bag into an open pan. Pour in the water and the fruit juice and boil for approximately 2 hours, or until the peel is tender. Once the peel is tender, test a little of the liquid for pectin (see page 26). Remove the bag and squeeze it well into the pan. Discard the bag and its contents.

5. Pour the granulated sugar into the pan and stir well using a wooden spoon. Continue stirring over a low heat until the sugar is dissolved, remembering to brush down the sides of the pan (see page 36). Rapidly boil the contents of the pan until setting point is reached.

6. To test if the marmalade has set, spoon a small amount onto a chilled saucer or conduct a flake test (see page 38). Add the whisky, then skim the top (see page 37) and then pour the boiling marmalade into jars and fill to 3 mm (⅛ in) below the brim. Wipe the outside and leave to cool. Label, date and store.

❧ Chinese Marmalade ❧

This marmalade smells suspiciously like Christmas, so will likely put you in a festive mood, whatever the time of the year.

680 g (1½ lb) golden plums, stoned and halved
150 ml (¼ pint) water
grated peel and juice of 1 lemon
grated peel and juice of 1 orange
900 g (2 lb) demerara sugar
900 g (2 lb) raisins, chopped or processed
60 g (2 oz) preserved ginger, chopped or processed
2 teaspoons brandy

1. Prepare the jars (see page 38).

2. Place the plums in a heavy saucepan, add the water and the lemon and orange peel and juice and cook until tender. Test for pectin (see page 26).

3. Pass through a sieve, then return the pulp to the pan and add the sugar and raisins. Cook slowly for 15 minutes. Add the ginger and boil quickly for 5 minutes. Test for set (see page 38). Pour the brandy over and stir in. Pot and seal immediately.

∞ *Grapefruit Marmalade* ∞

A sharp and bitter fruit that can be white, pink or red skinned, grapefruit makes for a wonderful marmalade. Generally speaking, the pinker the skin, the sweeter the fruit.

juice, peel and pith of 4 lemons
juice, peel and pith (only if thick) of 4 grapefruits
water to cover
680 g (1½ lb) of sugar to each 600 ml (1 pint) pulp

1. Prepare the jars (see page 38).

2. Place the pith, pips and any blemished pieces of peel into a muslin cloth and secure with a piece of string.

3. Chop the peel into strips of the required size and place in the preserving pan, together with the muslin bag. Pour in the water and fruit juice.

4. Simmer the contents of the pan for approximately 2 hours without a lid, or until the peel is tender and the liquid has reduced. Once the peel is tender, test a little of the liquid for pectin (see page 26). Remove the bag and squeeze it well into the pan. Discard the bag and its contents.

5. Pour the granulated sugar into the pan and stir well using a wooden spoon. Continue stirring over a low heat until the sugar is dissolved, remembering to brush down the sides of the pan (see page 36). Rapidly boil the contents of the pan until setting point is reached.

6. To test if the marmalade has set, spoon a small amount onto a chilled saucer or conduct a flake test (see page 38). Skim the top (see page 37) and then pour the boiling marmalade into jars and fill to 3 mm (⅛ in) below the brim. Wipe the outside and leave to cool. Label, date and store.

~ Apricot Marmalade ~

225 g (8 oz) dried apricots
juice, peel and pith of 340 g (12 oz) Seville oranges
juice and peel of 1 lemon
900 ml (1½ pint) water
1.5 kg (3 lb) granulated sugar
15 g (½ oz) split almonds

1. Soak the apricots for 12 hours in 600 ml (1 pint) water.

2. Prepare the jars (see page 38).

3. Finely shred the orange peel and tie the orange peel, pith and pips in a muslin bag.

4. Place the apricots, muslin bag and the remaining water in a heavy saucepan. Add the grated peel and strained juice of the lemon and simmer until tender, stirring occasionally. Remove the muslin bag, squeezing gently. Test for pectin (see page 26).

5. Add the sugar and stir until dissolved, then boil rapidly until setting point is reached (see page 38). Stir in the almonds. Pot and seal immediately.

❧ Carrot Marmalade ❧

Carrots are a sweet vegetable, but the addition of cinnamon to this preserve adds a greater depth of flavour. This twist on a classic recipe is delicious spread on scones or toast.

225 g (8 oz) carrots, peeled and finely chopped
juice, pith and peel of 225 g (8 oz) oranges
juice, pith and peel of 225 g (8 oz) lemons
1.75 litres (3 pints) water
½ teaspoon ground cinnamon
1.5 kg (3 lb) granulated sugar

1. Place the carrots in a heavy saucepan. Finely shred the orange and lemon peel. Place the pips and the pith in a muslin bag, tie up and add with the peel, water, juice and cinnamon to the carrots.

2. Simmer gently for 1½–2 hours until the peel is tender. Remove the muslin bag, squeezing gently. Test for pectin (see page 26).

3. Add the sugar and dissolve over a low heat, then boil rapidly until setting point is reached (see page 38). Skim and stir gently to disperse the peel. Pot and seal immediately.

JAMS

~ઓૅ~

A delicious home-made jam beautifully captures the taste of summer for your enjoyment at any time of the year. It is the ideal way to use a bumper crop of fresh fruit, but fruit can also be frozen and used when convenient (see page 29). Dried fruit may also be used. Sound, slightly under-ripe fresh fruit should be selected as this has the highest pectin content and it should be used as quickly as possible to maintain perfect condition. All fruit should be carefully washed and dried prior to use to remove any residue from spraying.

Well-made jam keeps perfectly, does not go mouldy and does not crystallize. It is clear and bright with a well-set texture that is not too stiff or rubbery. And in order to achieve a perfect set, there must be a correct balance of sugar, acid and pectin (see page 26). Most fruit preserves can be eaten after 24 hours – perfect for those people who can't wait to get stuck into their home-made produce.

Careful cooking of the fruit prior to adding sugar is also essential for good results. Cooking the fruit well ensures that the pectin is released, the skins are broken down and the juice is extracted. Hard-skinned fruits such as gooseberries, blackcurrants, plums and damsons require more water and a longer cooking time than soft fruits such as strawberries or raspberries.

Adding the sugar before the skins have softened will toughen them and adversely affect the texture of the finished jam.

The ideal saucepan for jam making has a heavy ground base and thick sides to prevent burning. If acid fruits are to be used, stainless steel, aluminium or enamel-coated saucepans must be used. Instructions for preparing the jars and for testing both for pectin and set are given in the preliminary section of this book, which should be studied carefully before commencing work.

Mary's Tip
The golden rule for jams is slow cooking before the addition of sugar, and very rapid, short boiling afterwards.

~e~ Rhubarb and Apple Jam ~e~

Tart and sweet, this jam sports a winning combination of flavours. Rhubarbs are low in pectin, so the addition of the apples is necessary to raise levels.

450 g (1 lb) cooking apples, peeled, cored
and sliced into 1 cm chunks
450 g (1 lb) rhubarb, washed, dried and
chopped into 1 cm chunks
juice of 1 lemon
900 g (2 lb) granulated sugar

1. Prepare the jars (see page 38).

2. Place the apple and rhubarb into a large saucepan with the lemon juice. Cover with a tightly fitting lid and simmer for 5–10 minutes, shaking the pan several times. Remove the lid and continue to cook until tender.

3. Add the sugar and stir over a low heat until dissolved. Brush down (see page 36). Turn up the heat and boil rapidly until setting point is reached, stirring occasionally. Check for set (see page 38).

4. Carefully pour the jam into jars, filling to the brim. Seal immediately, wipe down and leave to cool. Label and store.

~∞~ **Strawberry Jam** ~∞~

Home-made strawberry jam tastes better than any shop-bought version. Just be mindful of the fruit's low pectin content. See page 26 for more on pectin.

900 g (2 lb) strawberries, rinsed, hulls removed, cut into large pieces
juice of 1 lemon
750 g (1¾ lb) granulated sugar

1. Prepare the jars (see page 38).

2. Place the strawberries into a large saucepan and add the lemon juice. Heat gently, stirring constantly. Cook until the volume is slightly reduced, then conduct a pectin test (see page 26).

3. Add the sugar and stir over a low heat until dissolved. Brush down (see page 36). Turn up the heat and boil rapidly until setting point is reached, and remove any scum from the surface.

4. Test for set (see page 38). If ready, pour the jam into jars, filling to the brim. Seal immediately, wipe down and leave to cool. Label and store.

Mary's Tip

When making jams, always cook the fruit until soft before adding the sugar.

~๑๑~ **Blackcurrant Jam** ~๑๑~

Tart, tangy and simple to make, blackcurrant jam is an excellent recipe for a beginner as the fruit's high pectin content means the jam sets well.

450 g (1 lb) blackcurrants, rinsed and de-stemmed
500 ml (18 fl oz) water
900 g (2 lb) granulated sugar

1. Prepare the jars (see page 38).

2. Put half the blackcurrants into a liquidizer with half the water. Liquidize for a few seconds until the skins are broken. Pour into the saucepan. Repeat for the remaining fruit and water. Bring slowly to the boil and simmer gently for 5 minutes.

3. Add the sugar and stir over a low heat until dissolved. Brush down (see page 36). Boil rapidly, stirring occasionally until setting point is reached. Test for set (see page 38).

4. Remove any scum. Pour the jam into jars and fill to the brim. Seal immediately, wipe down and leave to cool. Label and store.

Mary's Tip
Liquidizing is particularly suitable for hard-skinned fruits, such as de-stoned plums and gooseberries, as the shorter cooking time needed retains the fruit's flavour.

❧ *Pineapple Jam* ❧

This delicious recipe adds a touch of the exotic to the world of jam. It tastes great spread on toast – add a scraping of cream cheese for extra depth of flavour.

250 g (9 oz) fresh pineapple, peeled and cut into small chunks
900 g (2 lb) cooking apples, peeled, cored and chopped
juice 1 lemon
150 ml (¼ pint) water
900 g (2 lb) sugar

1. Prepare the jars (see page 38).

2. Place the pineapple in a large saucepan with the water and the lemon juice. Simmer with the pan tightly covered until the pineapple is tender.

3. Drain the juice from the pineapple and add to the apple and simmer until tender. Add the cooked pineapple to the apple.

4. Add the sugar to the fruit and stir until dissolved. Brush down (see page 36). Boil hard until setting point is reached, stirring occasionally. Test for set (see page 38).

5. Carefully pour the jam into jars and fill to the brim. Seal immediately, wipe down and leave to cool. Label and store.

Mary's Tip
Always remove the saucepan from the heat when testing for pectin or set.

~⚬~ Seedless Blackberry and ~⚬~ Apple Jam

A classic combination of flavours, blackberries and apples are best enjoyed during the autumn. But remember you can freeze fruits when they are in season for use at a later date (see page 29).

900 g (2 lb) blackberries
150 ml (¼ pint) water
450 g (1 lb) cooking apples, peeled, cored and sliced
granulated sugar, as required: 450 g (1 lb) sugar to
450 g (1 lb) pulp

1. Prepare the jars (see page 38).

2. Place the blackberries in a saucepan with half the water and simmer until tender.

3. When tender, push the blackberries through a nylon sieve to remove the seeds. Place the apples in a covered pan with the remainder of the water and simmer until tender. Shake the pan several times during cooking.

4. Combine the cooked pulp of both fruits and weigh. Then weigh an equivalent amount of sugar.

5. Pour the pulp into a large, clean saucepan and add the sugar. Stir over a low heat until the sugar is dissolved. Brush down (see page 36) and boil until setting point is reached.

6. Test for set (see page 38). Pour the jam into jars and fill to the brim. Seal immediately, wipe down and leave to cool. Label and store.

Mary's Tip
The cooking time can be shortened by mashing the fruit during cooking.

~☙ Mixed Fruit Jam ☙~

An excellent recipe for when you have surplus quantities of fruit in the bowl. Feel free to experiment with the quantities of fruit, but remember that their combined weight should total approximately 900 g (2 lb).

blackcurrants
redcurrants
raspberries
blackberries
rhubarb, chopped into small chunks
apples, peeled, cored and chopped
= total weight approximately 900 g (2 lb)
900 g (2 lb) granulated sugar

1. Prepare the jars (see page 38).

2. Liquidize the blackcurrants for a few seconds to break down the skins. Then place the blackcurrants, redcurrants, blackberries and raspberries in a saucepan, cover and simmer gently until tender.

3. Place the apple and rhubarb in a separate saucepan, cover and simmer until tender.

4. Place all the cooked fruit in a large saucepan. Add the sugar and stir over a low heat until dissolved. Brush down (see page 36), then boil rapidly until setting point is reached (see page 38).

5. Test for set (see page 38). Pour the jam into jars and fill to the brim. Seal immediately, wipe down and leave to cool. Label and store.

Mary's Tip
Do not wash raspberries unless absolutely necessary as their juice will flow.

❧ *Apricot Jam* ❧

A classic French jam that is fairly straightforward to make.

> 900 g (2 lb) fresh apricots, washed,
> halved and de-stoned
> 150 ml (¼ pint) water
> 900 g (2 lb) granulated sugar

1. Prepare the jars (see page 38).

2. Carefully remove the kernels from a few apricot stones. Dip the kernels in boiling water and remove the skins.

3. Place the fruit and the kernels in a large saucepan with the water. Simmer until the contents are reduced by approximately one third.

4. Test for pectin (see page 26). Pour the pulp into a large, clean saucepan and add the sugar. Stir over a low heat until the sugar is dissolved. Brush down (see page 36) and boil until setting point is reached.

5. Test for set (see page 38). Pour the jam into jars and fill to the brim. Seal immediately, wipe down and leave to cool. Label and store.

❧ Cherry Jam ❧

A sweet and luscious jam that tastes delicious when spread on scones.

750 g (1¾ lb) dark cherries, pitted,
with the stones reserved
juice of 1 lemon
450 g (1 lb) granulated sugar

1. Prepare the jars (see page 38).

2. Carefully remove the stones from the cherries and weigh the fruit to the required amount.

3. Crush a few of the cherry stones and then tie them in a muslin bag together with the rest of the stones.

4. Place the cherries, muslin bag and lemon juice in a large saucepan. Simmer on a low heat until the cherries are tender. Remove the muslin bag.

5. Add the sugar and stir until dissolved. Brush down (see page 36), then boil rapidly until setting point is reached. Test for set (see page 38). Pot and seal immediately.

Mary's Tip
You can use a cherry pitter to remove the stones, but if you don't have one simply halve the cherries and take the stones out by hand.

❧ Rhubarb and Rose ❧ Petal Jam

Scented rose compliments sweet, tart rhubarb in this classic combination. Remember to use untreated rose petals – anything that has been sprayed could be toxic.

750 g (1¾ lb) rhubarb, washed and chopped
into thin slices
juice of 1 lemon
3 teacups rose petals
450 g (1 lb) granulated sugar

1. Pour the lemon juice over the rhubarb. Mix the sugar into the rhubarb (reserving 1 tablespoon) and cover the bowl with a plate. Leave to stand for 12 hours to allow the juice to flow.

2. Prepare the jars (see page 38).

3. Trim the white tip from each of the rose petals as these may be bitter and will spoil the delicate flavour of the jam. Finely chop the petals and sprinkle them with the reserved tablespoon of sugar.

4. Place the rhubarb and rose petals into a large saucepan, along with the sugar they have been resting in, and simmer until dissolved. Brush down (see page 36), then boil rapidly until setting point is reached. Pot and seal immediately.

Mary's Tip
Old-fashioned roses with a strong scent should be used for this recipe.

~ Gooseberry and ~ Elderflower Jam

As gooseberries reach their ripeness in mid summer, so too do elderflowers. The delicate, floral scent of elderflower and the sharp tang of gooseberries are a match made in heaven.

900 g (2 lb) young gooseberries
12 elderflower heads, rinsed, topped and tailed
water to cover
900 g (2 lb) granulated sugar

1. Prepare the jars (see page 38).

2. Thoroughly wash the elderflowers and trim from the stems. Tie the elderflowers into muslin.

3. Place the gooseberries and elderflowers in a pan and barely cover with water. Simmer until tender. Stir to prevent burning. The contents of the saucepan should be reduced by one third. Remove from the heat.

4. Remove the muslin bag and squeeze out all the juice.

5. Add the sugar and stir over a low heat until dissolved. Brush down (see page 36), then boil rapidly until setting point is reached (see page 38). Pot and seal.

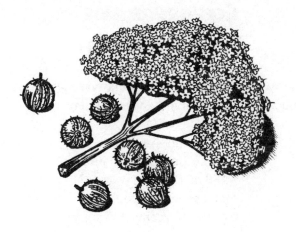

Mary's Tip
It's best to disturb the jam as little as possible
until it has cooled.

❧ Greengage and ❧ Bénédictine Jam

This grown-up jam marries plum-like greengages with Bénédictine, a herbal brandy-based liqueur.

450 g (1 lb) greengages
1½ tablespoons lemon juice
150 ml (¼ pint) water
3 tablespoons Bénédictine
680 g (1½ lb) granulated sugar

1. Prepare the jars (see page 38).

2. Prepare the fruit and place in a heavy saucepan with the water, lemon juice and Bénédictine. Boil for 15 minutes, stirring occasionally.

3. Add the sugar and dissolve slowly over a low heat, then boil until setting point is reached (see page 38). Skim if necessary, and pot and seal immediately.

⊶ Apricot and Amaretto Jam ⊷

Another alcohol-infused jam. In this recipe, the almond flavour of Amaretto is paired beautifully with sweet apricots.

900 g (2 lb) fresh apricots, washed, halved
and de-stoned
150 ml (¼ pint) water
900 g (2 lb) granulated sugar
3 tablespoons Amaretto

1. Prepare the jars (see page 38).

2. Carefully remove the kernels from a few apricot stones. Dip the kernels in boiling water and remove the skins.

3. Place the fruit and the kernels in a large saucepan with the water. Simmer until the contents are reduced by approximately one third.

4. Test for pectin (see page 26). Pour the pulp into a large, clean saucepan and add the sugar. Stir over a low heat until the sugar is dissolved. Brush down (see page 36) and boil until setting point is reached.

5. Test for set (see page 38). Stir in the Amaretto, then pour the jam into jars and fill to the brim. Seal immediately, wipe down and leave to cool. Label and store.

⊸⊶ High Dumpsie Dearie Jam ⊶⊷

This jam dates back to medieval times, when autumn fruits were collected together to create a preserve that would last through winter.

apples, peeled, cored and sliced
pears, peeled, cored and sliced
plums, peeled, cored and sliced
(fruit should measure in equal quantities, combined weight = 900 g (2 lb))
juice of 1 lemon
ground ginger, to taste
granulated sugar, as required: 340 g (12 oz) to 600 ml (1 pint) pulp

1. Prepare the jars (see page 38).

2. Place the fruit in a saucepan with a tightly fitting lid with a little water, the lemon juice and the ginger and cook slowly until tender.

3. Measure the pulp and add the appropriate amount of sugar. Dissolve slowly over a low heat, then boil rapidly until setting point is reached (see page 38). Pot and seal immediately.

~୬୦~ Blackberry, Apple and ~୬୦~ Rum Jam

This grown-up jam adds an alcoholic twist to a classic.

900 g (2 lb) blackberries
450 g (1 lb) cooking apples, peeled, cored and sliced
150 ml (¼ pint) water
granulated sugar, as required: 450 g (1 lb) sugar to
450 g (1 lb) pulp
1 tablespoon rum, or to taste

1. Prepare the jars (see page 38).

2. Place the blackberries in a saucepan with half the water and simmer until tender. When tender, push the blackberries through a nylon sieve to remove the seeds.

3. Simmer the apples in a covered pan with the remainder of the water until tender. Shake the pan several times during cooking.

4. Combine the cooked pulp of both fruits and weigh. Then weigh an equivalent amount of sugar.

5. Pour the pulp into a large, clean saucepan and add the sugar. Stir over a low heat until the sugar is dissolved. Brush down (see page 36) and boil until setting point is reached.

6. Test for set (see page 38). Stir in the rum and pour the jam into jars and fill to the brim. Seal immediately, wipe down and leave to cool. Label and store.

Mary's Tip

If jam has not set in 20 minutes, further boiling will result in spoiled flavour, hardening of skins and a syrupy texture.

‑ଓ‑ **Damson Jam** ‑ଓ‑

A species of plum, damsons are often reserved for cooking because their skin is quite tart in its uncooked state.

900 g (2 lb) damsons
300 ml (½ pint) water
1.5 kg (3lb) granulated sugar

1. Prepare the jars (see page 38).

2. Place the damsons and the water in a heavy saucepan and cook slowly until the fruit is tender and the contents slightly reduced.

3. Add the sugar and dissolve slowly over a low heat then boil rapidly until setting point is reached (see page 38), removing the stones with a slotted spoon as they surface. Remove further stones before potting if necessary. Pot and seal.

❧ *Plum Jam* ❧

Quick to make, this delicious jam makes a wonderful gift to give to friends and family.

1.5 kg (3 lb) plums
300 ml (½ pint) water
1.5 kg (3 lb) granulated sugar

1. Prepare the jars (see page 38).

2. Place the plums and the water in a heavy saucepan and cook slowly until the fruit is tender and the contents slightly reduced.

3. Add the sugar and dissolve slowly over a low heat then boil rapidly until setting point is reached (see page 38), removing the stones with a slotted spoon as they surface. Remove further stones before potting if necessary. Pot and seal.

～ Pear and Ginger Jam ～

The ginger in this recipe adds a kick to the mild taste and grainy texture of the pear.

900 g (2 lb) pears, peeled, cored and roughly chopped
juice, pith and peel of 2 lemons
450 ml (¾ pint) water
15 g (½ oz) ground ginger
900 g (2 lb) granulated sugar

1. Prepare the jars (see page 38).

2. Place the core and the peel of the pear together with the lemon pith and peel in a muslin bag.

3. Place the lemon juice, chopped pear and ginger in a saucepan with the water and cook for 10 minutes. Remove the bag, squeezing gently. Add the sugar and dissolve slowly over a low heat and then boil until setting point is reached (see page 38). Pot and seal immediately.

‑‑ *No-Cook Jam* ‑‑

The freezer can be used for storing this superbly flavoured, no-cook jam. It can be stored for up to 6 months.

680 g (1½ lb) raspberries or strawberries, crushed
1.25 kg (2½ lb) caster sugar
¾ bottle commercial pectin
3 tablespoons lemon juice

1. Place the fruit into a bowl and stir in the sugar. Leave to stand in a warm place for approximately 1 hour, stirring occasionally. Add the pectin and lemon juice and stir for 2 minutes.

2. Prepare the jars (see page 38). Alternatively you can use plastic containers.

3. Pour the fruit into small, dry jars, leaving a gap of 1 cm (½ in) below the rim. Cover and seal with foil or freezer-proof cling film and stand in a warm place for 48 hours. Label and freeze.

CURDS AND FRUIT CHEESES

Traditional country fare, curds have a unique creamy consistency that adds a touch of luxury to teatime. Curds are traditionally made from citrus fruits, and it's always best to use the unwaxed variety. If you can only find waxed, pour boiling water over them and give them a good scrub to remove the coating before cooking commences.

Curds are more perishable than jam as they contain butter and eggs. They should, therefore, be made in small quantities and stored in a refrigerator for up to 1 month. Free-range eggs with deep golden yolks produce a particularly rich-looking curd. It is important that curds should have a 'breathing' lid, such as cellophane, as this enhances the keeping properties and prevents mould forming.

A double saucepan should ideally be used for cooking, as the heat is more controllable, but a bain marie (see Mary's Tip) makes a good substitute if one is not available. Always ensure that the curd is really thick before potting as this produces its distinctive texture.

Fruit cheeses are also a traditional country food and can be served with cheese or as a delicious accompaniment to poultry, game or other meats. They are a useful way to use up a glut of fruit as the proportion of fruit used to produce a cheese is high, and the fruit

94

pulp that remains after the juice has been extracted for jelly making can also be used. The mould or jar, which can be a good polythene tub, should be smeared with glycerine so that the cheese can be easily turned out. A waxed cover should be used for the cheese top. Store the cheese in a cool, dry and dark place, and remember it will improve on keeping. The cheese is turned out from the pot and served in slices or wedges.

Apples, damsons, blackcurrants, cherries and quinces are particularly suitable for cheese making but cranberry cheese makes a tasty twist to serve with turkey. As with jam making, it is important to use sound, just-ripe fruit and to carefully wash and dry it before use to remove any pesticides.

Mary's Tip
A bain marie is a bowl placed on top of a saucepan of barely simmering water. It is used to heat ingredients gradually, so keep an eye on the water because you don't want to cook the ingredients too quickly.

✤ Lemon Curd ✤

A beautiful, rich and tangy preserve that is wonderfully easy to make.

85 g (3 oz) butter
peel of 4 lemons
150 ml (¼ pint) lemon juice
340 g (12 oz) granulated sugar
150 ml (¼ pint) eggs

1. Prepare the jars (see page 38).

2. Place the butter in a heatproof bowl and melt over a saucepan of boiling water. Add the lemon juice and peel and the sugar. Stir over the heat until the sugar is dissolved. When the sugar is dissolved, stand the bowl in cold water to cool.

3. In a separate bowl, beat the egg lightly without frothing.

4. When the butter and sugar mixture is cool, add it to the beaten egg, stirring well. Strain the mixture through a nylon sieve into a clean bowl.

5. Return to the heat by standing the bowl over a saucepan of hot water. Stir constantly until the mixture starts to thicken. When it's ready, the mixture should coat the back of a spoon. To test for thickness, run your index finger over the back of the covered spoon. If it's ready, a track should be left behind.

6. Pour the lemon curd into jars, filling to the brim, and immediately place a waxed disc on top.

7. When the lemon curd is cold, dampen cellophane in a saucer, on one side only, and place it, moist side up, onto the jar and secure with a rubber band. Label, store in the refrigerator and use as soon as possible.

Mary's Tip
Use a potato peeler to remove the lemon rind as the peel needs to be very thin.

~⚬~ *Apricot Curd* ~⚬~

A sweet twist on a classic, apricot curd is best enjoyed on toast or scones.

175 g (6 oz) dried apricots
water for soaking
60 g (2 oz) butter
juice and peel of 1 lemon
225 g (8 oz) granulated sugar
2 eggs

1. Soak the apricots for 24 hours in cold water.

2. Prepare the jars (see page 38).

3. Place the apricots in a saucepan and cook until tender. Sieve or liquidize to remove any lumps.

4. Place the butter in a heatproof bowl and melt over a saucepan of boiling water. Add the lemon juice, sugar and peel. Stir over the heat until the sugar is dissolved. When the sugar is dissolved, stand the bowl in cold water to cool.

5. In a separate bowl, beat the egg lightly without frothing.

6. When the butter and sugar mixture is cool, add it to the beaten egg, stirring well. Strain the mixture through a nylon sieve into a clean bowl.

7. Return to the heat by standing the bowl over a saucepan of hot water. Stir constantly until the mixture starts to thicken. When it's ready, the mixture should coat the back of a spoon. To test for thickness, run your index finger over the back of the covered spoon – if it's ready, a track should be left behind.

8. Pour the apricot curd into jars, filling to the brim, and immediately place a waxed disc on top.

9. When the apricot curd is cold, dampen cellophane in a saucer, on one side only, and place it, moist side up, onto the jar and secure with a rubber band. Label, store in the refrigerator and use as soon as possible.

~◦~ *Orange Curd* ~◦~

Orange curd makes a fabulously tart accompaniment to toast, crumpets, and all manner of other teatime treats.

115 g (4 oz) butter
juice and peel of 1 orange
115 g (4 oz) caster sugar
3 egg yolks

1. Prepare the jars (see page 38).

2. Place the butter in a heatproof bowl and melt over a saucepan of boiling water. Add the orange juice, peel and sugar. Stir over the heat until the sugar is dissolved. When the sugar is dissolved, stand the bowl in cold water to cool.

3. In a separate bowl, beat the egg yolks lightly without frothing.

4. When the butter and sugar mixture is cool, add it to the beaten egg, stirring well. Strain the mixture through a nylon sieve into a clean bowl.

5. Return to the heat by standing the bowl over a saucepan of hot water. Stir constantly until the mixture starts to thicken. When it's ready, the mixture should coat the back of a spoon. To test for thickness, run your index finger over the back of the covered spoon – if it's ready, a track should be left behind.

6. Pour the orange curd into jars, filling to the brim, and immediately place a waxed disc on top.

7. When the orange curd is cold, dampen cellophane in a saucer, on one side only, and place it, moist side up, onto the jar and secure with a rubber band. Label, store in the refrigerator and use as soon as possible.

～⊷ Gooseberry Curd ⊷～

Gooseberries reach the peak of their season in mid summer, but you can always freeze them to use at a later date (see page 29).

680 g (1½ lb) gooseberries, topped and tailed
300 ml (½ pint) water
60 g (2 oz) butter
340 g (12 oz) granulated sugar
2 eggs

1. Prepare the jars (see page 38).

2. Place the gooseberries in a pan with the water and simmer gently until soft. Sieve to remove the seeds.

3. Place the butter in a heatproof bowl and melt over a saucepan of simmering water. Add the sugar and stir over the heat until it dissolves. When the sugar is dissolved, stand the bowl in cold water to cool.

4. In a separate bowl, beat the egg lightly without frothing.

5. When the butter and sugar mixture is cool, add it to the beaten egg, stirring well. Strain the mixture through a nylon sieve into a clean bowl.

6. Return to the heat by standing the bowl over a saucepan of hot water. Stir constantly over the heat until the mixture starts to thicken. When it's ready, the mixture should coat the back of a spoon. To test for thickness, run your index finger over the back of the covered spoon. If it's ready, a track should be left behind.

7. Pour the gooseberry curd into jars, filling to the brim, and immediately place a waxed disc on top.

8. When the gooseberry curd is cold, dampen cellophane in a saucer, on one side only, and place it, moist side up, onto the jar and secure with a rubber band. Label, store in the refrigerator and use as soon as possible.

⚬ৡ Blackcurrant and Apple ৡ⚬ Cheese

This versatile cheese works just as well in a sponge as it does accompanied with cold meats.

1.5 kg (3 lb) cooking apples, cored,
sliced but skins kept on
450 g (1 lb) blackcurrants, de-stemmed
water, as required
granulated sugar, as required: 450 g (1 lb)
sugar to 450 g (1 lb) pulp

1. Prepare the jars (see page 38).

2. Place the fruit in a saucepan with sufficient water to barely cover. Simmer until tender and pulpy. Push the pulp through a nylon sieve.

3. Weigh the pulp and place it in a large saucepan with the appropriate amount of sugar. Dissolve the sugar over a low heat, stirring gently to prevent burning.

4. To test if the cheese is ready, draw a spoon across the bottom of the pan. If ready, a clean line will be formed. Pot into a warm container, such as a ramekin, coated with a thin layer of glycerine on the inside. Cover immediately with a wax disc and a cellophane cover.

‑◌‑ *Cranberry Cheese* ‑◌‑

Cranberries are delicious, autumnal berries that marry well with cheese and cold meats.

1.5 kg (3 lb) cranberries
water to cover
granulated sugar, as required:
450 g (1 lb) sugar to 450 g (1 lb) pulp

1. Prepare the jars (see page 38).

2. Place the fruit in a saucepan with sufficient water to barely cover. Simmer until tender and pulpy. Push the pulp through a nylon sieve.

3. Weigh the pulp and place it in a large saucepan with the appropriate amount of sugar. Dissolve the sugar over a low heat, stirring gently to prevent burning.

4. To test if the cheese is ready, draw a spoon across the bottom of the pan. If ready, a clean line will be formed.

5. Pot into a warm container, such as a ramekin, coated with a thin layer of glycerine on the inside. Cover immediately with a wax disc and a cellophane cover.

~ Damson Cheese ~

Sweet, dense and packed full of flavour, damson cheese is a wonderful accompaniment to game, but works just as well served as a dessert with a dollop of cream.

1.5 kg (3 lb) damsons
water to cover
granulated sugar, as required: 340 g (12 oz) to
450 g (1 lb) pulp

1. Prepare the jars (see page 38).

2. Place the fruit in a saucepan with sufficient water to barely cover. Simmer until tender and pulpy. Push the pulp through a nylon sieve.

3. Weigh the pulp and place it in a large saucepan with the appropriate amount of sugar. Dissolve the sugar over a low heat, stirring gently to prevent burning.

4. To test if the cheese is ready, draw a spoon across the bottom of the pan. If ready, a clean line will be formed.

5. Pot into a warm container, such as a ramekin, coated with a thin layer of glycerine on the inside. Cover immediately with a wax disc and a cellophane cover.

~ଊ৹ Quince Cheese ৹ଊ~

The fragrant taste of quince goes particularly well with cheese, especially Spanish manchego.

> 1.5 kg (3 lb) quinces, chopped with
> peel and core intact
> water to cover
> granulated sugar, as required:
> 450 g (1 lb) to 450 g (1 lb) pulp

1. Prepare the jars (see page 38).

2. Place the fruit in a saucepan with sufficient water to barely cover. Simmer until tender and pulpy. Push the pulp through a nylon sieve.

3. Weigh the pulp and place it in a large saucepan with the appropriate amount of sugar. Dissolve the sugar over a low heat, stirring gently to prevent burning.

4. To test if the cheese is ready, draw a spoon across the bottom of the pan. If ready, a clean line will be formed.

5. Pot into a warm container, such as a ramekin, coated with a thin layer of glycerine on the inside. Cover immediately with a wax disc and a cellophane cover.

～ Cherry Cheese ～

This sweet cheese tastes wonderful stirred into natural yoghurt.

1.5 kg (3 lb) cherries
water to cover
juice of 1 lemon
granulated sugar: 450 g (1 lb) to
each 450 g (1 lb) pulp

1. Prepare the jars (see page 38).

2. Place the fruit and the juice in a saucepan with sufficient water to barely cover. Simmer until tender and pulpy. Sieve the pulp through a nylon sieve.

3. Weigh the pulp and place it in a large saucepan with the appropriate amount of sugar. Dissolve the sugar over a low heat, stirring gently to prevent burning.

4. To test if the cheese is ready, draw a spoon across the bottom of the pan. If ready, a clean line will be formed.

5. Pot into a warm container, such as a ramekin, coated with a thin layer of glycerine on the inside. Cover immediately with a wax disc and a cellophane cover.

JELLIES

Jellies are made in a similar way to jams but are strained to produce a clear jelly-like texture with a distinctive bright and translucent colour and flavour. Only fruits that give a really good set are suitable for jelly making, as low pectin fruits may make the finished jelly cloudy and too runny.

The fruits selected for jelly making should be of the highest quality and slightly under-ripe to ensure the highest pectin content. As with all jam making, it is important to use the fruit as fresh as possible but fruit can be frozen until convenient (see page 29).

Little preparation is required for fruits for jelly making as the skins, cores and pips are discarded at the straining stage. However, the fruit should be carefully washed and dried before use and any blemishes removed. Fresh or frozen fruits can be used for jellies but an extra one-eighth weight of fruit should be used to compensate for any loss of pectin. If frozen citrus fruit is used for jelly marmalade, the fruit should be left to stand in a bowl of boiling water for 10 minutes. The oranges can then be cut in half and the flesh scooped out, or roughly chopped with a sharp knife.

When making jelly, cook the fruit slowly and thoroughly in order to release the pectin and to break down the fruit. When straining the cooked fruit through the jelly bag, don't squeeze or press the bag as otherwise the finished result will be cloudy. Suspending the bag will increase the rate of flow but at least one hour should be allowed for this process.

A jelly pan should be as heavy as possible, with a good base and thick sides to prevent burning. Stainless steel, aluminium or enamel-coated saucepans are ideal as the acid in the fruit does not react or taint the finished jelly.

The texture of a jelly bag is extremely important as too open a mesh will allow fruit tissue through and produce a cloudy jelly. It is advisable to purchase a purpose-made jelly bag for large quantities. However, if one is not available a close textured cloth can be utilized for a homemade bag. Muslin, or wine straining bags, should be avoided as the weave is too loose.

When filling jars with jelly, tilting the jars slightly will avoid bubbles forming. And for jellies, the smaller the jar, the better the setting that results.

∽ Marmalade Jelly ∽

While not quick to make, this jelly is so tasty it is worth putting in the extra effort. The additional peel also adds an interesting texture.

450 g (1 lb) Seville oranges
1.5 litres (2½ pints) boiling water
juice of 1 lemon
750 g (1¾ lb) granulated sugar

1. Prepare the jars (see page 38).

2. Place the oranges in a saucepan and cover with the water. Leave to stand for 2 minutes (or 10 minutes if using frozen fruit).

3. Remove the oranges from the water. Cut off the peel from one orange, remove the pith from the peel and cut the peel into very fine shreds. Place the shredded peel in a muslin cloth and secure with string.

4. Chop the remaining whole oranges into small pieces. Place the oranges, muslin bag, lemon juice and the water the oranges were steeped in into a pan. Cover with a tightly fitting lid and simmer gently for approximately 2 hours, or until the peel is tender.

5. Line a sieve with a piece of clean, fine cloth and place it over a heatproof bowl large enough to hold the contents of the pan. (Alternatively, use a jelly bag.)

6. Pour boiling water through the cloth to scald it and empty the water out of the bowl and discard. Remove the muslin bag and pour the contents of the pan into the cloth. Leave to strain. (The cloth can be suspended to increase the flow.)

7. Ensure that no pieces of fruit remain in the strained liquid. Test for pectin (see page 26).

8. Pour the liquid into a large pan and add the sugar. Dissolve the sugar over a low heat. Brush down (see page 36), then bring to the boil. Take the shredded peel out of the muslin bag and add it to the liquid. Boil until setting point is reached (see page 38). Skim if necessary (see page 37).

9. Carefully pour the marmalade into jars and fill to the brim. Seal immediately, wipe down and leave to cool. Label and store.

Mary's Tip
When potting jelly tilt the jar to avoid trapping bubbles.

⊸ Mixed Fruit Jelly ⊷

This recipe is a great way to use up surplus quantities of fruits. Almost all mixed berries give a very good flavour; why not try experimenting with different varieties.

raspberries
redcurrants
blackcurrants
loganberries
total weight of fruit = 2 kg (4 lb)
300 ml (½ pint) water
granulated sugar, as required: 450 g (1 lb) sugar to
600 ml (1 pint) juice

1. Prepare the jars (see page 38).

2. Place the fruit in a large saucepan with the water and simmer gently until tender. A masher can be used to release the juices from the berries.

3. Test for pectin (see page 26) and boil for a little longer if necessary.

4. Line a sieve with a piece of clean, fine cloth and place it over a heatproof bowl large enough to hold the contents of the pan. (Alternatively, use a jelly bag.)

5. Pour boiling water through the cloth to scald it and empty the water out of the bowl and discard. Pour the cooked fruit into the cloth and allow to drain. (The bag can be suspended to increase the flow.)

6. Measure the juice and weigh out the sugar. Pour the juice into a large saucepan and add the sugar and dissolve over a low heat, stirring gently. Brush down (see page 36), then boil rapidly until setting point is reached (see page 38). Pot and seal immediately.

Mary's Tip
Blackcurrants can be lightly liquidized before cooking. And remember to rinse all fruits in cold water before you begin.

⋙ Mint Jelly ⋘

The classic accompaniment to lamb, mint jelly is a sweet, delectable preserve that is straightforward to make.

900 g (2 lb) green gooseberries, tops and tails
left on
12 stalks fresh mint, washed
water to cover
granulated sugar, as required: 450 g (1 lb) sugar
to 600 ml (1 pint) of juice

1. Prepare the jars (see page 38).

2. Tie together 8 stalks of mint and place in a large saucepan along with the gooseberries. Pour in the water and simmer until well cooked.

3. Mash the gooseberries thoroughly and remove the mint if sufficient flavour has been imparted.

4. Line a sieve with a piece of clean, fine cloth and place it over a heatproof bowl large enough to hold the contents of the pan. (Alternatively, use a jelly bag.)

5. Pour boiling water through the cloth to scald it and empty the water out of the bowl and discard. Pour the mashed fruit into the cloth and allow to drain, but do not try to push the liquid through by forcing the fruit.

6. Measure the juice and weigh the appropriate amount of sugar. Pour the juice and sugar into a clean saucepan and dissolve slowly over a low heat. Finely chop the remainder of the fresh mint and add to the pan. Boil rapidly until setting point is reached (see page 38). Pot and seal immediately .

Mary's Tip

Try substituting the mint for thyme, sage, tarragon or rosemary. You can also add 1–2 drops of green edible food colouring before setting point is reached to enhance the colour of the jelly.

~ Lemon and Lime ~ Marmalade Jelly

A tart combination of fruits that produces a jelly perfect for spreading on buttered toast.

680 g (1½ lb) lemons
450 g (1 lb) limes
2 litres (3½ pints) boiling water
1.5 kg (3 lb) granulated sugar

1. Prepare the jars (see page 38).

2. Place the lemons and limes in a saucepan and cover with the water. Leave to stand for 2 minutes (or 10 minutes if using frozen fruit).

3. Remove the fruit from the water. Cut off the peel from one lemon and one lime, remove the pith from the peel and cut the peel into very fine shreds. Place the shreds in a muslin cloth and secure with string.

4. Chop the remaining whole fruit into small pieces. Place the fruit, muslin bag and the water the fruits were steeped in into a pan. Cover with a tightly fitting lid and simmer gently for approximately 2 hours, or until the peel is tender.

5. Line a sieve with a piece of clean, fine cloth and place it over a heatproof bowl large enough to hold the contents of the pan. (Alternatively, use a jelly bag.)

6. Pour boiling water through the cloth to scald it and empty the water out of the bowl and discard. Remove the muslin bag and pour the contents of the pan into the cloth. Leave to strain. (The cloth can be suspended to increase the flow.)

7. Ensure that no pieces of fruit remain in the strained liquid. Test for pectin (see page 26).

8. Pour the liquid into a large pan and add the sugar. Dissolve the sugar over a low heat. Brush down (see page 36), then bring to the boil. Take the shredded peel out of the muslin bag and add it to the liquid. Boil until setting point is reached (see page 38). Skim if necessary (see page 37).

9. Carefully pour the marmalade into jars and fill to the brim. Seal immediately, wipe down and leave to cool. Label and store.

❧ Clementine Marmalade ❧ Jelly

The distinctive and wonderfully sweet flavour of clementines is captured perfectly in this recipe. The fruit is in season during the winter months, so make sure you stock up then.

450 g (1 lb) clementines
juice of ½ grapefruit
juice of ½ lemon
1.5 litres (2½ pints) boiling water
1 teaspoon tartaric acid
680 g (1½ lb) granulated sugar

1. Prepare the jars (see page 38).

2. Place the clementines in a saucepan and cover with the water. Leave to stand for 2 minutes (or 10 minutes if using frozen fruit).

3. Remove the clementines from the water. Cut off the peel from one clementine, remove the pith from the peel and cut the peel into very fine shreds. Place the shredded peel in a muslin cloth and secure with string.

4. Chop the remaining whole clementines into small pieces. Place the clementines, grapefruit and lemon juice, muslin bag, tartaric acid and the water the clementines were steeped in into a pan. Cover with a tight-fitting lid and simmer gently for approximately 2 hours, or until the peel is tender.

5. Line a sieve with a piece of clean, fine cloth and place it over a heatproof bowl large enough to hold the contents of the pan. (Alternatively, use a jelly bag.)

6. Pour boiling water through the cloth to scald it and empty the water out of the bowl and discard. Remove the muslin bag and pour the contents of the pan into the cloth. Leave to strain. (The cloth can be suspended to increase the flow.)

7. Ensure that no pieces of fruit remain in the strained liquid. Test for pectin (see page 26).

8. Pour the liquid into a large pan and add the sugar. Dissolve the sugar over a low heat. Brush down (see page 36), then bring to the boil. Take the shredded peel out of the muslin bag and add it to the liquid. Boil until setting point is reached (see page 38). Skim if necessary (see page 37).

9. Carefully pour the marmalade into jars and fill to the brim. Seal immediately, wipe down and leave to cool. Label and store.

~ Gooseberry Jelly ~

Gooseberries make for a very tart but also sweet jelly.

900 g (2 lb) gooseberries
water to cover
granulated sugar, as required: 450 g (1 lb)
to 600 ml (1 pint) of juice
a handful of elderflower heads

1. Prepare the jars (see page 38).

2. Rinse the fruit and mince or process, then cook very slowly in the water until soft but not pulpy.

3. Test for pectin (see page 26) and boil for a little longer if necessary.

4. Line a sieve with a piece of clean, fine cloth and place it over a heatproof bowl large enough to hold the contents of the pan. (Alternatively, use a jelly bag.)

5. Pour boiling water through the cloth to scald it and empty the water out of the bowl and discard. Pour the cooked fruit into the cloth and allow to drain. (The bag can be suspended to increase the flow.)

6. Measure the juice and weigh out the appropriate amount of sugar. Pour the juice into a large saucepan and add the sugar. Dissolve over a low heat, stirring gently. Brush down (see page 36), then boil rapidly.

7. Place the elderflower heads in muslin and tie up with string. Add to the mixture three minutes before setting point is reached (see page 38). Remove the muslin bag, then pot and seal immediately.

~ Crab Apple Jelly ~

Crab apples are not normally available commercially, so you might have to raid a local orchard if you are not lucky enough to have a crab apple tree in your garden.

900 g (2 lb) crab apples, quartered along
with core and peel
water to cover
granulated sugar, as required: 450 g (1 lb)
to 600 ml (1 pint) of juice

1. Prepare the jars (see page 38).

2. Rinse the fruit and mince or process, then cook very slowly in the water until soft but not pulpy.

3. Test for pectin (see page 26) and boil for a little longer if necessary.

4. Line a sieve with a piece of clean, fine cloth and place it over a heatproof bowl large enough to hold the contents of the pan. (Alternatively, use a jelly bag.)

5. Pour boiling water through the cloth to scald it and empty the water out of the bowl and discard. Pour the cooked fruit into the cloth and allow to drain. (The bag can be suspended to increase the flow.)

6. Measure the juice and weigh out the appropriate amount of sugar. Pour the juice into a large saucepan and add the sugar. Dissolve over a low heat, stirring gently. Brush down (see page 36), then boil rapidly until setting point is reached (see page 38). Pot and seal immediately.

Mary's Tip
For extra flavour, add bruised ginger root, ground ginger or cloves to the fruit at step 2 in the recipe.

~∞~ Rose Jelly ~∞~

This delightful jelly builds on the recipe for Crab Apple Jelly on page 124. You'll get the best results if you use strongly scented, untreated petals – you don't want to end up with an upset stomach.

900 g (2 lb) crab apples, quartered along
with core and peel
water to cover
3 teacups rose petals
granulated sugar, as required: 450 g (1 lb) to
600 ml (1 pint) of juice

1. Prepare the jars (see page 38).

2. Rinse the fruit and mince or process, then cook very slowly in the water until soft but not pulpy.

3. Test for pectin (see page 26) and boil for a little longer if necessary.

4. Line a sieve with a piece of clean, fine cloth and place it over a heatproof bowl large enough to hold the contents of the pan. (Alternatively, use a jelly bag.)

5. Pour boiling water through the cloth to scald it and empty the water out of the bowl and discard. Pour the cooked fruit into the cloth and allow to drain. (The bag can be suspended to increase the flow.)

6. Measure the juice and weigh out the appropriate amount of sugar.

7. Trim the white tips from each of the rose petals as these may be bitter and will spoil the flavour of the jam.

8. Add the sugar, rose petals and a little water to a separate saucepan, dissolve over a low heat and simmer gently. Strain and add to the crab-apple juice, bring to the boil and boil rapidly until setting point is reached (see page 38). Pot and seal immediately.

Mary's Tip

Experiment with other edible flower petals – scented geranium, lemon, verbena, marigold and herbs are particularly suitable for this recipe.

⋘ Sloe and Apple Jelly ⋙

This jelly is delicious paired with game or strong cheese; it can also be used as a base for sauces to accompany red meat.

450 g (1 lb) sloes, roughly quartered with
peel and core intact
450 g (1 lb) cooking apples, roughly quartered
with peel and core intact
water to cover
granulated sugar, as required: 450 g (1 lb) to
600 ml (1 pint) juice

1. Prepare the jars (see page 38).

2. Mince or process the fruit, then cook very slowly in the water until soft but not pulpy. Test for pectin (see page 26) and boil for a little longer if necessary.

3. Line a sieve with a piece of clean, fine cloth and place it over a heatproof bowl large enough to hold the contents of the pan. (Alternatively, use a jelly bag.)

4. Pour boiling water through the cloth to scald it and empty the water out of the bowl and discard. Pour the cooked fruit into the cloth and allow to drain. (The bag can be suspended to increase the flow.)

5. Measure the juice and weigh out the appropriate amount of sugar. Pour the juice into a large saucepan and add the sugar. Dissolve over a low heat, stirring gently. Brush down (see page 36), then boil rapidly until setting point is reached (see page 38). Pot and seal immediately.

❧ Quince and Geranium ❧ Jelly

The japonica quince is high in pectin and makes a wonderful amber jelly, which is delicately fragrant when combined with scented geranium leaves.

900 g (2 lb) japonica quinces, washed and
roughly chopped
water to cover
granulated sugar, as required:
450 g (1 lb) to 600 ml (1 pint) juice
scented geranium leaves, as required:
2–3 to 600 ml (1 pint) juice

1. Prepare the jars (see page 38).

2. Place the fruit in a pan with the water and simmer gently until soft and pulpy. Test for pectin (see page 26) and boil for a little longer if necessary.

3. Line a sieve with a piece of clean, fine cloth and place it over a heatproof bowl large enough to hold the contents of the pan. (Alternatively, use a jelly bag.)

4. Pour boiling water through the cloth to scald it and empty the water out of the bowl and discard. Pour the cooked fruit into the cloth and allow to drain. (The bag can be suspended to increase the flow.)

5. Measure the juice and weigh out the sugar. Pour the juice into a large saucepan and add the sugar. Tie the geranium leaves in muslin and add to the juice and dissolve over a low heat, stirring gently. Brush down (see page 36), then boil rapidly until setting point is reached (see page 38).

Mary's Tip

It is essential you wash quinces thoroughly in order to remove the downy-like fluff on their skin.

⊶ *Bramble Jelly* ⊶

This jelly is a wonderful accompaniment to cheese and crackers.

900 g (2 lb) blackberries
water to barely cover
lemon juice, as required: 3 tablespoons to
600 ml (1 pint) juice
granulated sugar, as required: 450 g (1 lb) to
600 ml (1 pint) juice

1. Prepare the jars (see page 38).

2. Rinse the fruit and mince or process, then cook very slowly in the water until soft but not pulpy. Test for pectin (see page 26) and boil for a little longer if necessary.

3. Line a sieve with a piece of clean, fine cloth and place it over a heatproof bowl large enough to hold the contents of the pan. (Alternatively, use a jelly bag.)

4. Pour boiling water through the cloth to scald it and empty the water out of the bowl and discard. Pour the cooked fruit into the cloth and allow to drain. (The bag can be suspended to increase the flow.)

5. Measure the juice and weigh out the appropriate amount of sugar. Pour the juice into a large saucepan and add the sugar and the lemon juice. Dissolve over a low heat, stirring gently. Brush down (see page 36), then boil rapidly until setting point is reached (see page 38). Pot and seal immediately.

Mary's Tip
Make sure you pick new season, just ripe blackberries for this recipe.

‑‑ Spiced Tomato Jelly ‑‑

This savoury jelly works wonderfully with crab meat.

2 cloves
2.5 cm (1 inch) cinnamon stick
680 g (1½ lb) tomatoes, roughly chopped
450 g (1 lb) cooking or crab apples, roughly chopped,
peel and core intact
450 ml (¾ pint) water
115 ml (½ pint) malt vinegar
680 g (1½ lb) granulated sugar

1. Prepare the jars (see page 38).

2. Tie the spices in a muslin bag and place them in a pan with the tomatoes, apples and the water and stew until the mixture is soft. Remove the spices and sieve the tomatoes.

3. Add the vinegar and sugar and dissolve over a low heat, stirring gently. Brush down (see page 36), then boil rapidly until setting point is reached (see page 38). Pot and seal immediately.

Mary's Tip
Please note this recipe does not produce a clear jelly.

～⊙৩~ **Spiced Redcurrant Jelly** ~⊙৩~

The sharp and spicy flavour of this jelly suits a variety of red meats, and is a beautiful addition to lamb or venison casseroles.

2–3 cloves
2.5 cm (1 inch) cinnamon
680 g (1½ lb) redcurrants
450 ml (¾ pint) water
150 ml (¼ pint) malt vinegar
680 g (1½ lb) granulated sugar

1. Prepare the jars (see page 38).

2. Tie the spices in a muslin bag and place them in a pan with the redcurrants and water and stew until the mixture is soft. Remove the spices and sieve the redcurrants.

3. Add the vinegar and sugar and dissolve over a low heat, stirring gently. Brush down (see page 36), then boil rapidly until setting point is reached (see page 38). Pot and seal immediately.

Mary's Tip
Redcurrants are packed full of pectin, so this jelly should reach setting point with ease.

~⊙⊙~ *Quick Mint Jelly* ~⊙⊙~

This easy-to-make version of the classic jelly makes a wonderful accompaniment to roast lamb.

450 g (1 lb) green gooseberries
water to cover
granulated sugar, as required: 450 g (1 lb) sugar to
600 ml (1 pint) of juice
a bunch of fresh mint, tied

1. Prepare the jars (see page 38).

2. Place the gooseberries in a saucepan with the water and simmer until tender. Strain through a nylon sieve, pressing gently to push through the pulp.

3. Weigh the juice and add the appropriate amount of sugar and dissolve slowly over a low heat. Add the mint and boil rapidly until setting point is reached (see page 38). Remove the mint and pot and seal immediately.

Mary's Tip
Before you pot and seal the jelly, try adding a little extra chopped mint or some green food colouring.

CHUTNEYS

Chutneys can be very distinctive, and they add considerable zest to a meal and can give an imaginative touch to cold meats and cheeses.

Chutneys are made from a combination of fruit and vegetables added to vinegar, sugar and an array of spices. They are an excellent way of using up an over abundance of fruit or vegetables, and they keep very well. In fact, the flavour of chutneys improves with keeping, especially if you store them appropriately – they should always be left to mature in a cool, dark place for approximately 2–3 months before eating.

Chutneys are very much a matter of personal taste, some being hot and spicy, others mild and sweet. Careful balancing of the spices may be necessary in order to obtain just the right mix for your palate and notes should be kept for future reference. When adding hot spices, always err on the side of caution as the flavour can be extremely fierce. And always remember to label your jars to indicate whether the chutney is 'hot' or 'sweet'.

You can use up older, lower grade produce when making chutney, but make sure the fruits and vegetables you use are not blemished or mouldy, and always remember to wash and dry them carefully prior to use. Careful preparation of fruits and vegetables improves the finished texture of chutney, which should have a thick, jam-like consistency. The best results are obtained from finely chopping, mincing or processing (in a food processor) the ingredients and allowing them to cook slowly in an open pan to allow for evaporation of the moisture. Onions are usually softened separately. The chutney is ready when a spoon drawn across the saucepan leaves a track that does not fill with liquid.

Finally, it is vital you use the correct pan, suitable vinegar of a high quality and sterilized jars when making chutney as they are essential for good results and keeping qualities (see Tips and Tools on page 15).

Mary's Tip
Sultanas, crystallized ginger and chopped nuts give an added interest to the texture of a finished chutney.

~⊙~ Dried Apricot Chutney ~⊙~

This delicious chutney works wonderfully with cheese and cold meats. The recipe uses white spiced malt vinegar but you can also use white wine vinegar.

450 g (1 lb) dried apricots
water for soaking
450 g (1 lb) onions, chopped finely
115 g (4 oz) sultanas
1 dessertspoon whole pickling spice
3 pieces dried ginger root
1 teaspoon cinnamon
225 g (8 oz) granulated sugar
300 ml (½ pint) white spiced malt vinegar
1 teaspoon salt
juice and finely grated peel of 1 lemon
juice and finely grated peel of 1 orange

1. Pour sufficient water onto the apricots to cover and soak for 12 hours.

2. Prepare the jars (see page 38).

3. Drain the apricots in a sieve, reserving the liquid.

4. Place the onion in a saucepan and add a little of the apricot liquid. Cover with a tightly fitting lid and cook until tender.

5. Chop or mince the cooked apricots and sultanas and crush the spices and ginger root and tie into a muslin bag.

6. Dissolve the sugar in the vinegar in a large saucepan over a low heat. Place all the ingredients into the liquid, including the muslin bag of spices. Cook for approximately 1 hour or until the mixture is thick and smooth and there is no free vinegar (see page 37).

7. Remove the muslin bag. Pot while still hot, filling the jars to the brim, and stirring if necessary to remove air bubbles. Seal immediately and label when cool.

Mary's Tip

For a little bit of added texture, add 60 g (2 oz) of chopped walnuts before potting.

~oϿ~ Tomato and Apple ~oϿ~ Chutney

Both spicy and sweet, this chutney is an essential store-cupboard filler.

680 g (1½ lb) red tomatoes, skinned, de-seeded and roughly chopped
225 g (8 oz) onions, finely chopped
225 g (8 oz) white sugar
300 ml (½ pint) white malt vinegar
¼ teaspoon chilli powder
½ teaspoon ground ginger
450 g (1 lb) apples, peeled, cored and finely chopped or processed
1 teaspoon salt

1. Prepare the jars (see page 38).

2. Add the onion and a little of the juice from the tomatoes to a saucepan. Cover with a tightly fitting lid and cook until tender.

3. In a large saucepan, dissolve the sugar in the vinegar over a low heat.

4. Tie the spices in a muslin bag and add to the vinegar along with the rest of the ingredients.

5. Cook until the mixture is smooth and there is no free vinegar (see page 37). Remove the muslin bag and pot and seal immediately (see page 39). Label when cold.

Mary's Tip

When you chop the tomatoes, remember to reserve any of the excess juice. You can also rub any pulpy seeds through a sieve to capture any extra liquid, which can then be used to cook the onions.

~∞ *Hot Orange Chutney* ∞~

Something spicy and a little bit different to add to the mix, this chutney is a tasty accompaniment to all manner of meats and cheeses.

the juice and peel of 3 thin-skinned oranges
115 g (4 oz) onions, finely chopped
225 g (8 oz) dates
5 red or green chillies, cut in half and de-seeded
115 g (4 oz) granulated sugar
300 ml (½ pint) white distilled spiced vinegar
1 teaspoon ground ginger
1 teaspoon salt

1. Prepare the jars (see page 38).

2. Carefully remove the pith from the orange and discard.

3. Place the onions in a saucepan with half the orange juice and cook until tender.

4. Process the peel, flesh and the remaining half of the orange juice until smooth.

5. Add the chillies and the dates to the orange mixture and process until smooth. Alternatively, mince the chillies and dates separately.

6. Dissolve the sugar in the vinegar over a low heat. Add all the ingredients and cook until there is no free vinegar (see page 37). Pot and seal immediately. Label when cold.

Mary's Tip
When filling chutney or pickle jars, use a knife or a long-handled wooden spoon to remove air bubbles.

❧ Banana Chutney ❧

This is a great recipe for using up overripe bananas.

225 g (8 oz) onions, finely chopped
2 tablespoons water
145 g (5 oz) soft brown sugar
300 ml (½ pint) brown malt vinegar
900 g (2 lb) bananas, sliced thinly
2 teaspoons curry powder
1 teaspoon salt
60 g (2 oz) sultanas, finely chopped or minced
½ teaspoon cinnamon
¼ teaspoon pepper

1. Prepare the jars (see page 38).

2. Place the onions in a saucepan with the water. Cover with a tightly fitting lid and cook on a low heat until tender.

3. In a large saucepan, dissolve the sugar in the vinegar over a low heat. Add all the remaining ingredients and cook gently until smooth, stirring to prevent burning.

4. The mixture is ready when there is no free vinegar (see page 37). Pot and seal immediately. Label when cold.

MAKE YOUR OWN

~ಆ~ *Marrow and Apple* ~ಆ~ Chutney

This versatile chutney works well with almost everything.

900 g (2 lb) marrow, peeled, de-seeded and chopped
into small chunks
45 g (1½ oz) salt for layering
450 g (1 lb) cooking apples, peeled and roughly
chopped
225 g (8 oz) onion, peeled and roughly chopped
225 g (8 oz) sultanas
15 g (½ oz) whole mixed pickling spice
15 g (½ oz) root ginger
175 g (6 oz) soft brown sugar
900 ml (1½ pint) spiced vinegar

1. Layer the slices of marrow in a bowl,
sprinkling each layer with a bit of salt. Leave
for 12 hours, then drain and rinse.

2. Prepare the jars (see page 38).

3. Place the marrow, apple and onion into a
food processor along with half the sultanas
and process until smooth. Alternatively, these
ingredients can be minced or chopped.

4. Chop and thoroughly crush the pickling
spices and ginger using a heavy rolling pin
and tie into a muslin bag.

146

5. Place the processed ingredients in a large saucepan and add the sugar and vinegar. Stir over a low heat until dissolved.

6. Add the spice bag and the remaining whole sultanas and cook until tender and smooth and the contents have reduced by one third. The slower the cooking process, the darker the finished chutney will be. Pot, seal and label immediately.

Mary's Tip
Always keep a note of the amount of spices used in a chutney recipe and adapt next time, if necessary.

∽ Beetroot Chutney ∽

This fragrant chutney carries a hint of spice and works wonderfully as an accompaniment to cold meats and cheese.

680 g (1½ lb) beetroot
145 g (5 oz) onion, peeled and finely chopped
2 tablespoons water
85 g (3 oz) granulated sugar
450 ml (¾ pint) malt vinegar
2 cloves
1 teaspoon whole allspice
2 black peppercorns
145 g (5 oz) raisins, finely chopped or minced
1 teaspoon salt

1. Prepare the jars (see page 38).

2. Place the whole beetroots in a saucepan and cover with water. Cook until tender, then peel and chop, mince or food process finely.

3. Place the onion in a saucepan with the 2 tablespoons of water. Cover with a tightly fitting lid and cook until tender.

4. In a separate large saucepan dissolve the sugar in the vinegar over a low heat.

5. Crush the spices and tie into a muslin
bag and add to the vinegar along with the
remaining ingredients. Simmer until smooth
and there is no free vinegar (see page 37).
Remove the bag of spices and pot and seal.

MAKE YOUR OWN

❧ **Tomato Chutney** ❧

This is an old family recipe – delicious, hot and spicy.

450 g (1 lb) tomatoes, skinned, de-seeded and
roughly chopped
225 g (8 oz) onions, finely chopped
450 g (1 lb) demerara sugar
600 ml (1 pint) vinegar
6 red chillies, chopped
30 g (1 oz) grated ginger
450 g (1 lb) apples, peeled, cored and finely chopped
225 g (8 oz) sultanas
225 g (8 oz) marrow, peeled, de-seeded and chopped
into small chunks
2 teaspoons salt

1. Prepare the jars (see page 38).

2. Add the onion and a little of the juice from the
tomatoes to a saucepan. Cover with a tightly
fitting lid and cook the onion until tender.

3. In a separate large saucepan dissolve the
sugar in the vinegar over a low heat.

4. Tie the spices in a muslin bag and add to the
vinegar along with the rest of the ingredients.

5. Cook until the mixture is smooth and there is
no free vinegar. Remove the muslin bag and
pot and seal immediately. Label when cold.

☙ Gooseberry Chutney ☙

A delicious, tart relish that is fairly quick and easy
to make, but best if it is left to mature for at least 3
months.

600 ml (1 pint) malt vinegar
7 g (¼ oz) cayenne pepper
115 g (4 oz) mustard seeds
680 g (1½ lb) green gooseberries
450 g (1 lb) soft brown sugar
30 g (1 oz) salt
340 g (12 oz) raisins, finely chopped or minced
115 g (4 oz) currants, finely chopped or minced
30 g (1 oz) garlic, finely chopped or crushed

1. Prepare the jars (see page 38).

2. Place the vinegar in a large saucepan and add
   the cayenne pepper. Crush the mustard seeds
   gently with a rolling pin and add to the pan.

3. Add the gooseberries to the vinegar and cook
   until soft. Once soft, add the sugar and salt
   and dissolve slowly over a low heat. Sieve or
   food process the gooseberries.

4. Mix the sieved gooseberries with the raisins,
   currants and garlic. Bottle when cold.

~ Pumpkin Chutney ~

An ideal (and very quick) chutney to make at Halloween because after you have scooped the pumpkin flesh out of its skin, you can craft a devilish looking candle-lit lantern from the shell.

680 g (1½ lb) prepared pumpkin, roughly chopped
340 g (12 oz) tomatoes, roughly chopped
175 g (6 oz) onions, roughly chopped
60 g (2 oz) sultanas, roughly chopped
225 g (8 oz) soft brown sugar
225 g (8 oz) caster sugar
1 tablespoon salt
1 teaspoon ground ginger
1 teaspoon black pepper
1 teaspoon ground allspice
1 clove garlic, crushed
450 ml (¾ pint) white vinegar

1. Prepare the jars (see page 38).

2. Place all the ingredients in a large saucepan, bring to the boil and simmer gently until soft, smooth and there is no free vinegar (see page 37).

3. Pot and seal immediately.

~ Date and Apple Chutney ~

Sweet dates mix with tart apple in this delicious chutney.

1 onion, peeled and finely chopped
450 g (1 lb) apples, skinned and minced
450 g (1 lb) dates, minced
115 g (4 oz) demerara sugar
300 ml (½ pint) vinegar
½ teaspoon powdered mustard
½ teaspoon ground ginger
½ teaspoon cayenne pepper
½ teaspoon salt

1. Prepare the jars (see page 38).

2. Place the onion in a large saucepan with a little of the juice from the processed fruit and cook until tender.

3. Add the sugar, vinegar and the spices and dissolve over a low heat. Add the rest of the ingredients and cook until there is no free vinegar (see page 37). Pot and seal immediately. Label when cold.

∿ **Hot Indian Style Chutney** ∿

This tasty chutney is an ideal accompaniment to curry.

the juice and peel of 2 limes
225 g (8 oz) onions
450 g (1 lb) cooking apples, peeled,
cored and chopped
4 garlic cloves
30 g (1 oz) salt
450 g (1 lb) soft brown sugar
1.25 litres (2¼ pints) malt vinegar
2 chillies, de-seeded and processed
225 g (8 oz) raisins, finely chopped or processed
60 g (2 oz) powdered mustard
60 g (2 oz) ground ginger
2 teaspoons cayenne pepper

1. Prepare the jars (see page 38).

2. Carefully remove the pith from the lime peel and discard.

3. Place the onions in a saucepan with half the lime juice and cook until tender.

4. Process the skins, flesh and the remaining half of the lime juice until smooth.

5. Place the apples in a large saucepan and add the onions, processed limes, garlic, salt, sugar, vinegar and chillies and simmer until soft and well reduced.

6. Sieve or food process, then add the raisins and the remaining spices. Mix well, cover and leave to stand overnight in a warm place before potting. Allow to mature for at least 3 months before use.

Mary's Tip
Fruits for pickling need to be firm and sound but not necessarily of the finest quality.

~ Exotic Fruit Chutney ~

A quick and delicious chutney that incorporates the sweet and tangy flavours of a variety of delicious fruits.

450 g (1 lb) soft brown sugar
450 ml (¾ pint) white wine vinegar
450 g (1 lb) golden plums, skinned, de-stoned and roughly chopped
450 g (1 lb) fresh apricots, skinned, de-stoned and roughly chopped
1 small pineapple, skinned and roughly chopped
1 mango, skinned, de-stoned and roughly chopped
225 g (8 oz) peaches, skinned, de-stoned and roughly chopped

1. Prepare the jars (see page 38).

2. In a large saucepan dissolve the sugar in the vinegar over a low heat. Add all the remaining ingredients and cook gently until smooth, stirring to prevent burning.

3. The mixture is ready when there is no free vinegar (see page 37). Pot and seal immediately. Label when cold.

Mary's Tip
If necessary, adjust the amount of sugar to taste.

❧ Mango Chutney ❧

A quick and easy to follow recipe for a classic chutney.

6 or 7 ripe mangoes, peeled, de-stoned and roughly
chopped
150 ml (¼ pint) white vinegar
2 chillies, de-seeded and finely chopped
175 g (6 oz) demerara sugar
45 g (1½ oz) preserved ginger or
2 teaspoons ground ginger
2 garlic cloves, crushed
60 g (2 oz) raisins
¼ teaspoon salt

1. Prepare the jars (see page 38).

2. Place the mango in a large saucepan, add the vinegar and simmer for approximately 10 minutes, or until tender.

3. Add the chillies and the sugar, dissolving slowly over a low heat. Simmer until the mixture begins to thicken, then add the spices, raisins and the salt. Cook for a further 30 minutes until smooth and there is no free vinegar (see page 37). Pot and seal immediately.

~ Damson Chutney ~

This delicious chutney goes well with almost anything.

1.5 kg (3 lb) damsons
2 onions, roughly chopped
115 g (4 oz) dates, de-stoned
225 g (8 oz) raisins
1 clove garlic, crushed
1 teaspoon salt
1 teaspoon ground ginger
1 teaspoon ground allspice
1 teaspoon cinnamon
1 litre (1¾ pint) malt vinegar
680 g (1½ lb) demerara sugar

1. Prepare the jars (see page 38).

2. Place the damsons in a large saucepan with the onions, dates, raisins, garlic, salt and spices. Add the vinegar and sugar and simmer until soft and very thick with no free vinegar (see page 37).

3. Remove the damson stones as they rise to the surface. Pot and seal immediately .

Mary's Tip
Remember to rinse and dry the fruit thoroughly before you commence cooking.

⊸ *Pepper Chutney* ⊸

This is an easy chutney to make and tastes delicious with cheese and cold meats.

1 teaspoon crushed mustard seed
1 teaspoon allspice
1 teaspoon crushed peppercorns
9 red, green and yellow peppers (3 of each colour),
de-seeded and finely chopped
450 g (1 lb) ripe tomatoes, skinned and roughly
chopped
340 g (12 oz) onions, roughly chopped
450 g (1 lb) cooking apples, peeled, cored and
roughly chopped
225 g (8 oz) demerara sugar
600 ml (1 pint) malt vinegar

1. Prepare the jars (see page 38).

2. Tie the spices in a muslin bag and place in a large saucepan along with the rest of the ingredients. Simmer on a low heat for at least 1½ hours, or until smooth and there is no free vinegar (see page 37).

3. Pot and seal immediately.

⊷ *Plum Relish* ⊷

This is an ideal barbecue relish and should be eaten within 2 months of making.

900 g (2 lb) red plums
4 onions, peeled and kept whole
300 ml (½ pint) vinegar
340 g (12 oz) demerara sugar
12 crushed peppercorns
2 chillies
6 cloves
2 teaspoons salt
1 teaspoon mixed spice

1. Prepare the jars (see page 38).

2. Place the whole plums and the whole onions in a large saucepan along with the rest of the ingredients. Bring to the boil then simmer gently until the mixture is smooth and there is no free vinegar (see page 37).

3. Remove the whole onions and allow to cool, and remember to remove any plum stones that have risen to the surface.

4. Sieve or blend the onions in a food processor until smooth. Add to the mixture and boil for a further 5 minutes. Pot and seal immediately.

ᨳ Gooseberry Relish ᨳ

This piquant relish should be eaten within 2 months of making.

680 g (1½ lb) gooseberries, topped and tailed
150 ml (¼ pint) malt vinegar
900 g (2 lb) granulated sugar

1. Prepare the jars (see page 38).

2. Place the gooseberries in a large, heavy saucepan with the vinegar and half of the sugar. Simmer gently until soft.

3. Add the remainder of the sugar and simmer until the mixture becomes syrupy. Pot and seal immediately.

PICKLES

~ↄ℮ↄ~

ickles are a time-honoured way of preserving a wide variety of fruits, vegetables, nuts and seeds. Use good quality, young, even-sized crisp vegetables and just-ripe fruit and carefully wash and dry before use. If handling vegetables such as beetroot or walnuts, remember to wear rubber gloves to prevent your hands from being stained.

Pickling recipes often call for brining, which is used to extract some of the moisture in certain vegetables (which is then replaced by the vinegar during processing). After vegetables have been brined, they should be rinsed thoroughly under cold running water to remove the salt and then drained well as water will weaken the vinegar and result in an inferior pickle.

Vegetables for sharp pickles are left uncooked but sweet pickles, particularly fruit, are usually cooked gently in spiced vinegar and then bottled in sweetened vinegar syrup. Vegetables such as beetroot may require hot vinegar as this enhances the keeping properties, but crisp vegetables require cold vinegar. Care should be taken when packing the vegetables into jars not to press them down too tightly as the vinegar needs to surround each piece, and air bubbles should be avoided by tapping the jar or stirring the contents slightly. As the pickles tend to absorb the vinegar, it may be necessary to top up the jars with vinegar after a day or two.

Vinegar is the most important ingredient of pickles and should be of the best quality with an acetic acid content of at least 5 per cent. (The draught variety of vinegar can be low in acetic acid.) Extra flavour is added to pickling vinegar by infusing it with herbs or spices, and wine vinegars can impart a delicate taste to many pickles. Please see page 23 for more advice on choosing the right vinegar.

Enamel-lined or stainless steel pans and glass bowls are ideal for pickling as other metals may impart a distinctive tang; nylon and plastic sieves should be used for the same reason. It is essential to use jars with airtight, vinegar-proof lids (which are either lacquered all over the inside or are made from plastic). Jars can be reused but care should be taken to ensure that suitable lids are used (these are available from specialist outlets if required).

Most pickles require keeping in a cool, dark place for a minimum of 6 weeks, but preferably 2 to 3 months to allow the flavours to mature – it will be worth the wait.

~ಆಾ~ **Mixed Pickles** ~ಆಾ~

This menagerie of pickled vegetables should be ready to eat after 2 or 3 months.

115 g (4 oz) salt
1 litre (1¾ pints) water
red and green peppers, diced
small onions or shallots, whole
cauliflower florets, diced
courgettes, diced
marrow, diced
green beans, sliced
cucumber, diced
total weight of vegetables = 900 g (2 lb)
spiced white vinegar, as required (see page 23)

1. Make the brine by dissolving the salt in the water. Place the vegetables in a large bowl and cover with the brine. Place a plate on top to keep them submerged and leave to soak for 48 hours.

2. Prepare the jars (see page 38).

3. Place the vegetables in a sieve and rinse under cold running water. Drain thoroughly.

4. Pack the vegetables into jars, taking care not to compress. Fill the jars to the brim with cold spiced-vinegar. Pot, seal and label and remember to top up with vinegar after 2 or 3 days, if necessary.

⤝ Pickled Red Cabbage ⤞

This classic pickle is ready to eat after 2 or 3 weeks, but be mindful of its shelf life – the cabbage will lose its crispness after approximately 2 months.

1 medium- to large-size whole red cabbage,
finely chopped
salt for layering
spiced vinegar, as required (see page 23)

1. Place a layer of the red cabbage in a large basin and sprinkle with salt. Continue layering and salting the cabbage until all the cabbage is used. Place a plate on top of the cabbage to weigh it down and leave it for 24 hours.

2. Prepare the jars (see page 38).

3. Place the cabbage in a nylon sieve and drain. Rinse well under cold running water and then drain thoroughly.

4. Loosely pack the cabbage into jars and fill to the brim with cold spiced-vinegar. Seal the jars and top up with vinegar after two or three days, if necessary. Label.

Mary's Tip
Red wine vinegar can be used instead of spice vinegar. And be wary not to compress the cabbage down into the jars.

·⊙· **Spiced Pickled Prunes** ·⊙·

These tasty prunes are delicious served with pâté and will be ready to eat after 3 or 4 weeks.

225 g (8 oz) prunes
water, as required
300 ml (½ pint) wine vinegar
4–5 cloves
2 × 50 mm (2 inch) cinnamon stick
225 g (8 oz) demerara sugar

1. Soak the prunes in water for 12 hours.

2. Prepare wide-necked jars (see page 38).

3. Drain the prunes and discard the water.

4. Pour the vinegar into a large saucepan and add the cloves and cinnamon. Dissolve the sugar in the vinegar over a low heat. Add the prunes and simmer until tender. Try to avoid breaking the prune skins.

5. Carefully remove the prunes from the liquid and pack into jars. Return the vinegar to the heat and boil until reduced to a syrupy consistency. Pour the syrup over the prunes and fill to the brim. Seal the jars and prepare additional syrup if required.

Mary's Tip
You can leave the cinnamon stick in whichever jar it lands in. It will enhance the flavour of the prunes with keeping.

❧ *Spiced Oranges* ❧

These delicious spiced oranges will be ready to eat after 6 to 8 weeks and taste delicious with cold meats, especially ham.

3 large sweet oranges, scrubbed and thickly sliced
into 6 mm (¼ inch) rounds
water to cover
450 g (1 lb) granulated sugar
300 ml (½ pint) white wine vinegar
5 cm (2 inch) cinnamon stick
5 cloves
3 blades of mace

1. Prepare wide-necked jars (see page 38).

2. Put the oranges into a saucepan and add just enough water to cover. Simmer for approximately 1½–2 hours, or until the skins are tender. Carefully remove the cooked oranges from the saucepan and drain in a nylon sieve.

3. Dissolve the sugar in the vinegar over a low heat. Add the spices and boil for 5 minutes. Add the oranges, cover and cook for a further 30 minutes, by which point their skins should be transparent. Carefully remove the cooked oranges and drain in a nylon sieve.

4. Boil the syrup until thick. Layer the oranges in jars and cover with the syrup, ensuring no air is trapped between the layers. Prepare additional syrup if necessary. Seal and label.

Mary's Tip
Pears, peeled, cored and sliced lengthwise, can be substituted for the oranges in this recipe.

~ *Piccalilli* ~

This is a fairly mild version of the classic preserve. It should be ready to eat after 3–4 months.

60 g (2 oz) salt
600 ml (1 pint) water
cucumber, diced
green beans, diced
cauliflower, diced
marrow, diced
courgettes, diced
small onions or shallots, peeled and left whole
total amount of vegetables = 450 g (1 lb)
35 g (1¼ oz) white sugar
1 teaspoon turmeric
¼ teaspoon ground ginger
1 teaspoon powdered mustard
300 ml (½ pint) distilled malt vinegar
7 g (¼ oz) cornflour

1. Make the brine by dissolving the salt in the water. Place the vegetables in a bowl and cover with brine. Submerge with a plate and leave to stand for 24 hours. Drain and rinse, then drain again thoroughly.

2. Prepare the jars (see page 38).

3. In a large saucepan add the sugar, the spices and two thirds of the vinegar and dissolve over a low heat. Add the vegetables and simmer until the desired texture is reached. Please note, the vegetables can be crisp, but not hard, or tender but not mushy.

4. Stir the cornflour into the remaining vinegar then add to the saucepan with the vegetables and boil for 2–3 minutes. Fill jars to the brim, avoiding air pockets by tapping the jar gently. Seal and label.

～ Pickled Onions ～

Pickled onions are a versatile, tasty and popular snack.
These should be ready to eat after 3–4 months.

115 g (4 oz) salt
1 litre (1¾ pint) water
450 g (1 lb) shallots or small onions,
outer skins removed
spiced vinegar, as required (see page 23)

1. To make the brine, dissolve the salt in the
water. Place the onions in a bowl and cover
with the brine. Submerge with a plate and
leave to stand for 24 hours for small onions,
or 36 hours for larger onions.

2. Prepare the jars (see page 38).

3. Drain the onions in a sieve, rinse well under
cold running water and then drain again
thoroughly.

4. Put the onions into jars, leaving a 1 cm (½ inch)
space at the top of each jar. Fill to the brim with
cold spiced-vinegar and seal immediately. Top
up with vinegar after 2–3 days if necessary.

Mary's Tip
The yellow sulphur marks that may develop on
pickled onions are harmless.

✺ *Chunky Vegetable Pickle* ✺

This tasty pickle will be ready to eat after 2 months and will keep well if stored in a cool, dry and dark place.

225 g (8 oz) carrots, diced
600 ml (1 pint) spiced malt vinegar (see page 23)
200 g (7 oz) demerara sugar
225 g (8 oz) courgettes (zucchini), diced
225 g (8 oz) onions, diced
340 g (12 oz) cauliflower, diced
450 g (1 lb) cooking apples, diced
115 g (4 oz) sultanas
3 tablespoons tomato purée
2 tablespoons lemon juice
2 tablespoons orange juice
1 clove garlic, crushed
½ teaspoon ground mixed spice

1. Prepare the jars (see page 38).

2. Place the carrots in a saucepan with a little salted water and boil for 4 minutes. Drain well in a sieve.

3. Pour the vinegar into a large saucepan and add the sugar. Stir over a low heat until the sugar is dissolved.

4. Add the remaining ingredients to the vinegar and cook uncovered for approximately 1 hour, or until the contents are reduced. Pot and seal immediately.

~ꙮ~ *Pickled Nasturtium Seeds* ~ꙮ~

These caper-like seeds taste delicious when pickled. This recipe does not specify the amount of nasturtium seeds needed because the quantity picked depends on how much you'd like to pickle, not to mention how much is available.

nasturtium seeds, carefully washed
60 g (2 oz) salt
600 ml (1 pint) water
cold spiced white vinegar (see page 23)

1. To make the brine, dissolve the salt in the water. Place the nasturtium seeds in a bowl and cover with the brine and leave to stand for 12 hours.

2. Prepare the jars (see page 38).

3. Drain the seeds and pack into jars leaving a 1 cm (½ inch) gap at the top. Cover with cold spiced-vinegar and seal immediately. Leave to mature for at least 1 month.

Mary's Tip
For best results, pick the nasturtium seeds on a dry day.

‑‑ *Pickled Walnuts* ‑‑

Traditionally eaten on Boxing Day with cold turkey and bread sauce, pickled walnuts are also a delicious accompaniment to any cold meats or cheese. This recipe does not specify the quantity of walnuts needed – just pickle however many you can lay your hands on.

60 g (2 oz) salt
600 ml (1 pint) water
green walnuts
cold spiced or sweet vinegar (see page 23)

1. Dissolve the salt in the water to make the brine. Place the walnuts in a bowl and cover with the brine and leave to stand for 3–4 days.

2. Change the brine and soak the walnuts for a further 7 days.

3. Drain the walnuts and spread on trays. Expose the walnuts to the air until they become black, which should take approximately 24 hours.

4. Prepare the jars (see page 38).

5. Pack the walnuts into the jars and cover with spiced or sweet vinegar. Seal immediately and leave to mature for at least 1 month.

Mary's Tip

Walnuts for pickling must be gathered while the shells are still soft and green – to test for softness prick the end opposite the stalk with a needle or silver fork and discard any walnuts that are hard.

Always wear rubber gloves when handling walnuts as their stain is very persistent and difficult to remove.

~⚬⟩⚬~ Runner Bean Pickle ~⚬⟩⚬~

A popular garden vegetable, runner beans taste wonderful when pickled.

450 g (1 lb) runner beans, stringed and sliced
2–3 large onions, peeled and roughly chopped
1 cooking apple, peeled and roughly chopped
450 g (1 lb) demerara sugar
450 ml (¾ pint) vinegar
1 tablespoon cornflour
1 tablespoon turmeric
½ teaspoon mustard

1. Prepare the jars (see page 38).

2. Place the runner beans in a saucepan of salted boiling water and cook until soft. Drain thoroughly.

3. Place the onions and a little water in a separate saucepan with a tightly fitting lid and cook until tender. Meanwhile, place the apple in another separate saucepan with a tightly fitting lid and cook until tender.

4. Place the sugar, apple and half the vinegar into a large saucepan and boil for 15 minutes. Mix the rest of the ingredients with the remaining vinegar and add to the mixture. Boil for a further 15 minutes. Pot and seal immediately.

～ Pickle Sticks ～

This is an extremely attractive pickle and makes a useful accompaniment to cold meats or cheese at a buffet. Allow to mature for 6–8 weeks before eating.

115 g (4 oz) salt
1 litre (1¾ pint) water
carrots, peeled and cut into matchstick-size pieces
celery, cut into matchstick-size pieces
cucumber, cut into matchstick-size pieces
courgette (zucchini), cut into matchstick-size pieces
French beans, cut into matchstick-size pieces
red, green, yellow peppers, cut into
matchstick-size pieces
total weight of vegetables = 900 g (2 lb)
spiced vinegar, as required (see page 23)

1. Make the brine by dissolving the salt in the water. Place the vegetables in a large bowl and cover with the brine. Place a plate on top to keep them submerged and leave to soak for 48 hours.

2. Prepare the jars (see page 38). Place the vegetables in a sieve and rinse under cold running water. Drain thoroughly.

3. Pack the vegetables into jars, taking care not
to compress. Fill the jars to brim with cold
spiced-vinegar. Seal and label and remember
to top up with vinegar after 2 or 3 days, if
necessary.

~ Mustard Pickle ~

This is a spicy pickle that should be allowed to mature for 6 weeks before eating.

115 g (4 oz) salt
1.5 litres (2½ pint) water
175 g (6 oz) cucumber, cut into large chunks
175 g (6 oz) onion, peeled and cut into large chunks
225 g (8 oz) cauliflower, cut into large chunks
115 g (4 oz) green tomatoes, peeled and cut into large chunks
340 g (12 oz) green peppers, cut into large chunks
225 g (8 oz) runner beans, cut into large chunks
225 g (8 oz) gherkins, sliced
225 g (8 oz) granulated sugar
22 g (¾ oz) mustard seeds
900 ml (1½ pint) vinegar
a pinch of turmeric
15 g (½ oz) powdered mustard
30 g (1 oz) plain flour

1. Make the brine by dissolving the salt in the water. Place the vegetables and the gherkins in a large bowl and cover with the brine. Soak for 12 hours.

2. Prepare the jars (see page 38).

3. Drain the vegetables thoroughly and chop roughly (or food process if a smooth pickle is required). Place vegetables in a pan with the sugar, mustard seeds and most of the vinegar, and bring to the boil.

4. Make a paste from the remaining vinegar, spices and flour and add to the vegetable mixture. Stir while bringing back to the boil, then simmer uncovered for approximately 20 minutes, or until tender. Pot and seal immediately.

Mary's Tip

A sweet version of this pickle can be made in the same way by substituting 60 g (2 oz) sultanas for the mustard.

⟡ *Pickled Pears* ⟡

Pack these tasty treats into attractive jars and give them as Christmas presents. Ensure you allow the pears to mature for 1 month before eating.

900 g (2 lb) sugar
300 ml (½ pint) sweet, spiced white vinegar
(see page 23)
900 g (2 lb) firm pears, peeled, cored and quartered

1. Prepare the wide-necked jars (see page 38).

2. In a large saucepan dissolve the sugar in the vinegar. Add the pears and simmer gently with a lid on until the pears are tender then pack into warm jars.

3. Boil the syrup until it becomes thick, pour over the pears and seal immediately.

186

INDEX

INDEX